US university scholarships for international students

The comprehensive guide to undergraduate financial aid and funding at America's top-ranked institutions.

GW00777622

by Steve Fenoglio
Mayflower Education Consultants Ltd.

Published by Mayflower Education Consultants Ltd.
10 The Birches
Goring-on-Thames
Oxfordshire, UK
RG8 9BW

info@mayflowereducation.co.uk

ISBN 978-0-9574205-0-2

Book Disclaimer

We have made every effort to produce and communicate accurate information for this edition of <u>US university scholarships for international students</u>. Decisions regarding scholarships and admission are the sole responsibility of the specific university, agency or organization and their employees. Therefore, parties associated with this book cannot guarantee any positive outcomes regarding awards or admission decisions. This book is strictly a guide. We assume neither responsibility nor liability regarding the contents of this book.

Acknowledgements

This book would not have been possible without the support of many people who have inspired me along the way. My colleagues and friends who have assisted me throughout include Matt Rader, Rachael Todt, Nicole and my colleagues at the Fulbright Commission.

Special thanks to Alison Cooper for her stellar work researching and compiling large amounts of information into a single, comprehensive database.

Also, this book is dedicated to my parents, John and Judy Fenoglio, who allowed me to continue my university education without a monetary worry in the world. I realize now how lucky I was to receive that support and care.

Last of all, to my darling wife, who has really made this all possible with her unwavering love and wonderful sense of humour.

Table of Contents

Information and education are powerful forces in support of peace.

-Dwight D. Eisenhower

1. Introduction

There are important reasons, both personal and professional, for writing this book. Professionally, as an education consultant in the UK, I work with hundreds of international students (and parents) who would love to study in America. Growing up there, I negotiated the admission process with relative ease, having followed the path laid out by my siblings and friends. Having now viewed the process through the eyes of my international clients, I appreciate the complexity of the system and the view of it from abroad. This book aims to explain and solve many of the mysteries relating to the US admissions and *financial aid* processes.

Personally, I believe global education and student mobility are critical to making the world a more peaceful place. While studying in a foreign land, students learn that knowledge, empathy and cultural understanding do not have to be political in nature or a major undertaking. It can occur one student at a time.

For the majority of students, financial assistance is, understandably, a very important consideration. The good news is there are funds available and this book details how those funds can be accessed. The Mayflower Education Consultants team can also offer assistance to guide you through the admissions and financial aid processes.

When reading about US financial aid, terminology is often confusing, given the various meanings of words, the reader's country of origin and the multiple sources of information. This book is written for international students (and parents) interested in attending university (usually four years) in the United States to earn an undergraduate degree, also known as a Bachelor of Arts (B.A.) or Bachelor of Science (B.S.). By international, I mean the interested student is neither a US citizen nor a permanent resident (green card holder) and has no legal right to funds offered by the US government for educational purposes. Nor do they have any legal right to work in the United States as a son or daughter of a permanent resident.

All of the scholarships, programmes and aid listed in this book are available to international students.

Students are completing their A-levels, International Baccalaureate(IB), Baccalauréat, Abitur, Vestibular or similar and plan on attending a university in the US as an international undergraduate student for the fall (autumn) term after high school. Most every US institution prefers, and may even mandate, that international students begin at the start of the academic year (i.e. August/September). The best time to start reading this book is at the beginning of a student's penultimate academic year of high school, or sooner if possible.

It is important to note that on US university campuses, international student applications are viewed differently than US nationals. The reason for these 'different lenses' is due to various government acts (i.e. student visas), university limitations (i.e. capacity) or the university mission (i.e. state laws). International students are assessed with respect to English language ability, the rigor of their home high school curriculum, grades, financial need and so on.

Prior to continuing, I strongly recommend you review the **Glossary** section of this book. The terms used throughout this book are listed there and in the first instance, are *italicised*. A good understanding of the vocabulary will ease the overall process in the search for funding. I have also added black labels (shown below) for particularly note-worthy facts.

Important

When searching university websites, make sure that the information you are reading pertains to international students. University web sites often link to pages that do not necessarily apply to the audience of the previous page. For example, some international office websites will link to the general student financial aid information, not specifically international student aid. If you are not sure of a particular programme or detail, ask for clarification by sending an email to either the international admissions office or the financial aid office of the university. Most schools will respond quite quickly.

In the United States the terms 'university' and *'college'* are virtually interchangeable, and in this book, they mean and refer to the same thing; a four year institution. If the word 'community' or 'technical' appears in front of the word 'college' that generally means a two year institution.

Not discussed in this book is the English language requirement as it pertains to US admission. It is, however, required for every student from a country whose legal language is not English. While most US universities offer student support for English as a second language, neither a university offer nor a visa will be issued to a student who has not achieved the university English requirement. English skills are assessed by taking either a *TOEFL* (Test of English as a Foreign Language) or *IELTS* (International English Language Testing System) exam.

For reference, in the 2010-2011 academic year, the annual average tuition for a US public institution was $13,600 and $36,300 at a US private institution. (U.S. Department of Education, 2011).

2. What does a US university offer?

Attending university in the United States is a unique experience. Not only does it introduce students to a new culture, ethos and even diet, but it also offers different methods of learning, both academically and personally. It can be difficult to summarise the many talents and skills acquired while studying abroad, however, the Institute for the International Education of Students has done extensive research on the subject (Gillespie 2002). Here are some of their findings:

- 98% of students reported that the study abroad experience helped them to better understand their own cultural values and biases

- 96% indicated that it increased self-confidence

- 76% said they acquired skill sets that influenced their career path

> For the seventh year in a row, the University of California at Los Angeles (UCLA) leads U.S. institutions in international student enrolment, with New York University coming in second. (IIE 2011).

Tens of thousands of students are drawn to US institutions each year. Undoubtedly, world-class academics are the main reason. In the most recent Times Higher Education rankings, 14 of the top 20 institutions in the world are in the United States. (TSL Education 2012). However, there are other aspects of US university life that attract international students. Last year more than 720,000 international students studied in the US. (IIE 2011). Additional reasons for studying at an American university may include:

- The liberal arts education
- Facilities and activities
- Work visas and employment

The Liberal Arts Education

Choice is at the heart of US higher education. Compared to many countries, America offers incredibly flexible university degrees and without question, this is one of the most popular reasons students attend university in America. By choice, I mean that students applying to university in the United States do not have to declare a discipline or specific area of study, known as a *major,* before applying or being accepted. For students who are not exactly sure what discipline they want to study at university, this is particularly good news. For international students, the liberal arts curriculum will be considerably different from other well-known higher education systems. Students have the independence to choose many of the classes necessary to complete graduation requirements, as opposed to following a path dictated by the institution. This holistic approach requires that all students take a variety of classes, often known as *general education requirements,* in order to provide an underpinning for future studies or success in the workplace. According to Harvard University,

> "the liberal arts education 'heightens students' awareness of the human and natural worlds; makes them more reflective about their beliefs and choices, more self-conscious and critical of their presuppositions and motivations, more creative in their problem-solving, more perceptive of the world around them, and more able to inform themselves about the issues that arise in their lives, personally, professionally, and socially". (Harvard University 2009).

The liberal arts curriculum can be described as an education which promotes an understanding of various scientific, philosophical and social schools of thought, preparing students to understand the world around them. Along with learning specific details associated with a discipline or subject area, a liberal arts education aims to teach students how to think rationally and logically. The University of California Berkeley describes the liberal arts education further as "laying the foundation for a future career while also preparing you to compete in the marketplace of ideas. It "frees your mind and helps you connect dots you never noticed before, so you can put your own field of study into a broader context". (University of California Berkeley 2012).

American universities have developed a curriculum that incorporates broader subject areas, as a requirement for all undergraduates. Generally, most universities require undergraduate students to complete two terms of English, an ethics class, a science class with a lab component, two social science classes and possibly a history class or meet a foreign language requirement in order to graduate. The exact class requirements will vary from institution to institution. For example, most universities in the state of Texas require students to take a Texas history class.

A few institutions in America still require a swimming test as a graduation requirement. They include Columbia, Bryn Mawr, M.I.T, Cornell, Notre Dame, Swarthmore and Dartmouth.

As noted earlier, these classes are typically referred to as general education requirements or GenEd's. They are also called area requirements, liberal arts requirements, foundation classes or the common curriculum, depending on the institution. Each university will call it something different, but it represents the same thing: liberal arts classes necessary to meet the university requirements for graduation.

In addition to these general education requirements, most US universities will allow students to take additional open *electives*. Students are able to enrol in any class, as long as the prerequisites for that class are met. This allows students significant flexibility in fulfilling the *degree* requirements.

The University of North Carolina at Chapel Hill Bulletin states:

"All entering UNC students spend the first two years in the General College. During these four semesters they are required to take a variety of courses in English, foreign language, mathematics, natural sciences, social sciences, aesthetics, history and philosophy. These classes are required by each and every undergraduate student at the University. In the opinion of university officials and academics, this repertoire of classes prepares the graduates for the job market and facilitates graduates who are holistic and have a basic understanding of numerous disciplines and areas of study. The second two years are focused on the student's major" (University of North Carolina at Chapel Hill 2012).

The other important aspect of the liberal arts education is the ability to enter university without declaring a *major*. Students at US institutions are able to apply and may begin their college careers without declaring exactly what discipline they will study. This is known as an undecided *major* or undeclared. Students generally take two years of general education requirement classes before having to declare a major. Allowing students to choose their major later allows two things to occur, both of which benefit the student. First, if the student is interested in a few different subject areas and cannot make a decision between them, the US system allows the flexibility to try a few and choose at a later date. The general education requirements will give students additional insight into their academic interests or introduce new ones. This flexible curriculum gives students the time to decide on their major. Secondly, universities in the US allow students to change their mind, even if a major has been declared. As general education requirements are necessary for every undergraduate degree awarded by an institution, students can embark on a new direction and apply the previously completed general education requirements to their new major, saving time and money. Of course, students will be required to fulfil the requirements of their new major, but the general education requirements will not need to be repeated.

Activities and Facilities

Activities

Another reason a student may choose an American university is the wide range of activities that are available to every member of the university community. From sports and recreation facilities to gaming and language labs, academic, social or interest organisations, US universities offer opportunities for students to investigate almost any interest they may have. The list is practically endless, but if students cannot find organisations that fit their interest, the university is typically happy to help establish one.

Sports are very popular on US university campuses. Sports teams exist in three different categories. The highest competitive level or *varsity* is of great interest to the university. For the top 500 universities, sports scholarships or bursaries help athletes attend the university and play a particular sport. These competitions are played at a very high level and many varsity athletes go on to professional sports careers. The second competitive level, club teams, is generally comprised of athletes who played a particular sport in high school. Club teams often play against the varsity teams in practice. Finally, there are intramurals. These are sports teams that any student can join and are organised and facilitated by the university.

> When the University of Nebraska Cornhuskers play football at their home stadium, the stadium becomes the state's third largest city.

Along with sports teams, there are music groups, language clubs, debate teams, religious organisations, student government, slow food groups, model UN chapters, computer societies, Greek fraternities and sororities and many others. Beloit College, a small school of 1250 students in southern Wisconsin, has over 100 student organisations. (Beloit College 2012). Larger schools like UCLA or the University of Michigan will have over a thousand student groups and clubs. Students enrolled in the university are able to pursue membership to any club which is recognised by the University. It is illegal in the US to exclude anyone on the basis of race, religion, colour or disability.

Facilities

Given the competitive nature of higher education in the US, institutions have developed state-of-the-art facilities as a means of differentiation. This benefits the entire community, especially students. Performance halls, sports stadiums, athletic facilities, IT labs, science labs, green space, dining facilities are all areas where US institutions take an enormous amount of pride and invest considerable resources.

Music, voice and theatre students will have access to campus music rooms in order to practice their craft. Student accounts, including class registration, class handbooks, recorded lectures, professors' websites, housing assignments and employment opportunities are all online and easily accessible. Most campuses offer wireless internet access across the entire campus. Dining facilities will have options for all types of tastes including vegan, kosher and halal meals. Various fast-food chains are popular on campus as are banks, bookstores, art galleries, dry cleaners and post offices. Sports facilities are often where universities try to make the biggest impression, and therefore, much of the equipment will be of high quality. You can watch TV while you cycle or have a go at the three-storey rock climbing wall. Most institutions will assist in keeping you healthy with wellness programmes and exercise classes.

Georgia Tech's Campus Recreation Centre (CRC) has been voted the best US student athletic facility by the Princeton Review. It offers 15,000 ft² of exercise area, a 50 metre pool with a 180 ft. slide and 16-person spa, a 39-foot climbing wall, studios for aerobics courses and beach volleyball courts. (Georgia Institute of Technology 2012).

Work Visas and Employment

Another advantage to studying in the US is the ability to legally work in the country during and after university. Working in the United States is allowed for authorized F-1 visa holders; however, there are many rules to consider prior to accepting employment. During the academic year, international students are currently permitted to work on campus for up to 20 hours per week while school is in session. During school breaks or holidays, students can work full-time.

Additionally, there are two types of work permits for students: optional practical training (OPT) and curricular practical training (CPT). CPT is work that is associated with a student's area of study, such as an internship or work placement and takes place before the student has graduated. CPT must take place off-campus, not begin before a student has studied at the institution for at least one year and be associated with a specific course at the university. CPT can be part-time or full-time, however, students working for 12 months full-time on CPT lose their eligibility for OPT.

OPT (optional practical training) is full-time employment which typically begins after your studies are completed. An international student must apply for OPT, have health insurance and the work must be related to your field of study. Regular OPT can last for up to one year, unless your field of study is in the STEM subjects (science, technology, engineering and math) which allows students to extend their OPT up to an additional 17 months for a possible total of 29 months. In order to qualify for this extension, students must have studied in one of the following disciplines:

- Actuarial Sciences
- Computer Science Applications
- Engineering & Engineering Technologies
- Life Sciences

- Mathematics
- Military Technologies
- Physical Sciences

After the optional practical training period, students have 60 days in order to prepare for departure from the United States. For details about all of the university's work authorisation schemes, contact the university's international office. They will be the best source for information, jobs or internships.

> The most popular major at US institutions is business.
> The highest earning major is biomedical engineering.

3. What type of institution is best for you?

With over 4400 US institutions (National Center for Education Statistics 2011) granting degrees at an associate level or higher including Bachelor's, Master's and Doctorate degrees, international students have a vast variety of schools from which to choose. The following descriptions will help you develop a list of the type of institution to which you may apply. US higher education institutions are often described or classified in many ways: academic, athletic, public or private.

Academic divisions

Higher education colleges and universities in America carry many types of academic classifications, based mainly on the overall mission of the institution.

Private universities

Most of the well-known US universities are private. Currently 14 of the top twenty American universities are privately funded and managed. This includes all of the *Ivy League* schools. Private universities determine their own admission criteria, price, curriculum, degree requirements and campus policies. These institutions are also particularly good at raising funds for their *endowment*, which they are able to spend with fewer restrictions compared to their public university counterparts. Many will help able, yet poorly funded students with financial assistance in the form of aid or *grants*. Private institutions award Bachelor's and Master's degrees and some will also award Doctoral degrees. Along with the Ivy League, some other well-known private institutions include the University of Southern California (USC), the University of Chicago and the University of Notre Dame.

Public universities

Public institutions, on the other hand, have less independence and take more direction from the state in which they are located. Public institutions are granted funds and resources from the state treasury. In their infancy, public universities were typically granted a large tract of land, in exchange for the state authorisation to grant degrees. For example, the University of Michigan was granted a large tract of land from the City of Ann Arbor, Michigan (The Regents of the University of Michigan 2012). States often mandate other requirements which may include, but are not limited to, lower tuition fees for in-state students or residents, requiring a curriculum consistent with the state charter and developing an ongoing and equitable relationship with the community.

The names of universities will often give you a good indication of their classification too. Usually, universities with the word "State" or "Tech" in their title are a public university (Arizona State, Iowa State and Texas Tech fit into this category) or the University of *State name* (Florida, Georgia, Montana etc.). This is not always the case as MIT (Massachusetts Institute of Technology) is private. Public institutions award Bachelor's, Master's degrees and Doctoral degrees.

Research or Teaching-based institutions

The culture of an institution can be influenced by its focus on research or teaching and this designation further differentiates US universities. Research-based and teaching-based universities offer the same liberal arts curriculum but the focus of the *faculty* work outside of the classroom may differ.

Students interested in research or scientific methods may find a research institution more to their liking. Institutional or private funding will be granted to the university for the duration of a research project undertaken by its faculty. Students are often involved with such projects and research will be at the heart of the academic programmes. Columbia University, Johns Hopkins University and Stanford University are well-regarded research institutions.

Teaching-based institutions value the interaction between student and professor, and identify best practices for teaching excellence. Students at a teaching institution will have flexible access to their professors, some of whom may live in the same residence hall and/or participate in other school activities such as leading the debate team. Dartmouth College, Princeton University and Miami University in Ohio are institutions highly ranked for teaching. However, these descriptions are not mutually exclusive. Many research-based institutions have talented faculty who are very involved with students and meet with them regularly. Most every four year institution will have office hour requirements for their faculty. Likewise, a teaching institution will also be involved in research in which students can often take part. These classifications refer to the main focus of the institution, but not its overall activities.

Community colleges

Community colleges have changed tremendously over the past decade. Originally, community colleges targeted the local community, similar to technical colleges. Now, however, community colleges offer a wide variety of degrees and classes with a few awarding four-year degrees, South Texas College, for example. Community colleges have transitioned from being small relatively unknown institutions to large popular schools attracting students from all over the world. In fact, some community colleges are challenging the long held belief that 2-year community colleges are academically inferior to 4-year universities. There is some research that shows a graduate from Cascadia College performs better academically in the third year of university than a typical (one who did not attend a community college) third-year student at the University of Washington in Seattle. (Carey 2009).

Choosing a community college can be one way to secure a place more easily and reduce costs and these colleges are growing in popularity. We will speak more about utilising the community college as a method to reduce the overall cost in further chapters, but here are some common community college characteristics. Community colleges will typically have lower admission requirements than four year institutions, less housing and a larger local commuter population. They will also often have *articulation agreements* with local four year institutions easing *credit* transfer from the community college to the four year university. Community colleges will typically specialize in a vocation or a highly focused curriculum. Miami-Dade College (MDC), the largest community college in the country offers a highly specialized funeral services education programme (Miami-Dade College 2012), but MDC also offers degrees in the liberal arts areas including Journalism, Philosophy and Political Science.

According to the American Association of Community Colleges, there are about 91,000 international students enrolled in community colleges in the United States. (AACC 2012).

Technical Colleges

Technical colleges offer courses and degrees in specific vocational disciplines. These may include degrees in automotive maintenance, heating, ventilation and air conditioning (HVAC) or video production, for example. These are typically two year degrees and campuses do not normally offer housing nor many, if any, extra-curricular activities.

Technical colleges may sound similar to community colleges, but have two distinct differences. 1) Technical colleges will not offer any liberal arts classes. English, history or social science requirements will be neither required nor available at a technical college. 2) Four-year institutions do not typically accept credit from technical colleges.

Athletics

Another way universities differentiate themselves is through athletics. These classifications are made independent of the academic classification of the university. There are three main athletic regulatory bodies in the US and the main difference between them is the number and type of member schools. They are:

- National Collegiate Athletic Association (NCAA)
  - 1280+ members, three divisions and the governing sports body for the majority of institutions in America (National Collegiate Athletic Association 2012).

- National Junior College Athletic Association (NJCAA)
  - 525 members and serves more than 60,000 student athletes. (National Junior College Athletic Association 2012).

- National Association for Intercollegiate Athletics (NAIA)
  - 300 members mostly smaller universities throughout North America (National Association for Intercollegiate Athletics 2012).

Each association offers national championships and support for student athletes and fosters a very high level of athletic competition. The NAIA and NCAA are made up of colleges and universities. The NJCAA is made up of community colleges. The NCAA also hosts the NCAA Men's Basketball Championship each year (commonly known as The Final Four) and honours strong student-athletes as Academic All-Americans.

The NCAA is divided into three divisions. The divisions of the NCAA are based on the number of co-ed sports teams the University supports and attendance levels.

Division I is comprised of the largest schools and the most widely known institutions. Division I schools:

- support at least seven men's and seven women's sports teams
- meet certain audience attendance requirements
- offer sports scholarships

Division II is comprised generally of medium-size schools. Division II schools:

- support at least ten sports, five each for men and women
- offer some sports scholarships

Division III is comprised of smaller institutions. Division III schools:

- support at least ten sports, five each for men and women
- offer no sports scholarships

It is easy to think that the largest schools (by student population) are Division I and the smaller schools are Division II or III. However, this is not always the case. The University of California San Diego is a leading public academic institution with approximately 30,000 students. It is however, Division II, athletically speaking.

Originally the Ivy League was so named as a sports conference whose members 'possessed ivy on their buildings walls'. Since then, many other conferences have been established given the large number of schools participating in intercollegiate athletics. The membership in these conferences is constantly changing. For example the Big Ten Conference, originally formed of ten large Midwestern institutions like the University of Michigan, the University of Illinois and the University of Chicago is now made up of 12 teams, but it's still called the Big Ten, and stretches from Pennsylvania to Nebraska. A selection of ten universities made up the PAC 10 Conference for many years, but it has recently changed to the PAC 12 and includes universities from Colorado to California.

Student-athletes interested in sports scholarships must be aware of the specific rules and regulations issued by the NCAA regarding academic and athletic eligibility. There are scholarships available to top performers; however, competition for this type of *merit-based aid* is extremely high. It must also be noted that Division III schools and the Ivy League institutions do not offer athletic scholarships.

Athletic Scholarships

Many international students are interested in attending an American university in order to play sports, and earn an athletic scholarship. In order to qualify for an athletic scholarship, most universities require the student-athlete to be competing at a very high level in their home country. Athletes should be ranked nationally or, at the very least, be participating in regional championships. Assessing an athlete's suitability is one of the most difficult tasks so it is recommended to speak with a knowledgeable coach. Student-athletes must also be pursuing a high school or equivalent degree and retain their amateur status, which typically means neither collecting prize money for competitions nor hiring an agent.

The top university coaches are assessing student-athletes two or more years prior to entering university. For many international athletes, it may be worth considering smaller universities and colleges in the NAIA or NJCAA. There are more opportunities with smaller institutions and they often have more flexible recruiting rules.

Student-athletes should assemble a sports curriculum vitae or resume, including physical characteristics (height, weight, age) a list of sports teams, awards and personal best times, if appropriate. Upload videos of your performances to YouTube and add the link. Also include academic strengths, test scores and intangibles such as work ethic, skills and leadership qualities. Send this sport resume to coaches at institutions where you honestly believe you can compete. Personalise the letter and be brief, highlighting how you could fit into their team. Sports to consider for US scholarships include American football, athletics (track & field), basketball, golf, tennis, rowing (crew), football (soccer) and rugby. International students must also remember that they are competing against student-athletes from all around the world, including America.

Sports are also big business in the United States. In 2010, the top 15 college football programmes generated over $1 billion in combined revenue. (Memphis Journal 2012). Below are the ten largest stadiums, in terms of seating capacity, in college football. Most of them sell out every Saturday afternoon.

1. Beaver Stadium (Pennsylvania State University)	107,282
2. Michigan Stadium (University of Michigan)	106,201
3. Ohio Stadium (Ohio State University)	102,329
4. Darrell K. Royal-Texas Memorial Stadium (University of Texas)	100,119
5. Neyland Stadium (University of Tennessee)	100,011
6. Rose Bowl (UCLA)	95,000
7. L.A. Memorial Coliseum (USC)	93,607
8. Sanford Stadium (University of Georgia)	92,746
9. Tiger Stadium (LSU)	92,400
10. Bryant-Denny Stadium (University of Alabama)	92,138

(The New York Times Company 2012).

4. Admissions and financial aid overview

Admissions overview

The admission process for US universities is unique. It requires dedicated planning, thoughtful consideration and a lot of writing. The process outlined below is similar across most US universities.

Students will generally apply to an American university at the start of their final year of high school. For each US institution, students will need to complete a separate admissions application. Students can submit an application through the *Common Application* (commonapp.org) or via the university's own website before the applicable institutional deadline. US universities set their own deadlines which vary considerably, and charge an application fee which typically ranges from $50 to $125 per school. Paper applications are possible, but discouraged. (More costs associated with applying are listed in Appendix 3).

Along with the actual admission application, international students will generally need to supply their *grades, SAT or ACT* exam scores (if required), teacher references, and a *personal statement*. Some of the top-ranked universities also require an admission application supplement or additional SAT subject tests. Applicants must request that their high school send grades directly to the university admission office. ACT or SAT exams are taken during final term of the penultimate year of high school or the first term in the final year of high school. These scores are sent by the testing company directly to the university as designated by the student. The application materials collected by the university or college will present a picture of each student to the admissions staff, from which they will make an admission decision. A well-organised, error-free and complete application will give international students the best possibility of gaining admission to the institution.

If offered admission, international students will be required to confirm their acceptance by a certain date, usually in early Spring. A non-refundable deposit is usually required by the university indicating the student's intent to enrol. Further information will be communicated by the university regarding the US *student visa*, financial aid, start dates and payment information. All international students must have US health insurance which is required by both the US government and the university. Each university will have a preferred provider. If you are unclear about any requirements or deadlines, contact the university admissions office or check their website.

Financial Aid Overview

'Financial aid' in the US is a very general term. It can mean many things, including funds given to students who cannot meet the financial requirements (need-based aid), scholarships awarded to talented, gifted students (merit-based aid) or loans (usually taken out through the US government) to meet the obligations of the university. It is very important to understand what type of aid is available and what aid an international student can actually apply for. It varies greatly. International students do not qualify for US government loans; therefore, I will address the other two types of financial aid offered by institutions for international students: need-based aid and merit-based aid.

Need-based Aid

Need-based aid is university financial assistance for students who cannot meet the financial obligations of the university. An international student's ability to qualify for need-based aid at a US *need-aware university* is always based on two criteria: The applicant pool that they are applying with (i.e. the other students applying for financial aid at the given institution) and the amount of funding available from that university.

An international student applying for need-based aid is required to provide financial information to the university or college proving their inability to pay. Exactly what financial information to send and when to send it depends on the type of institution and their available funds for international students. With regards to need-based aid, there are three types of institutions:

1. Need-aware institutions that award need-based aid
2. *Need-blind* institutions that award need-based aid
3. Institutions that do not award any need-based aid

Of the top ranked 100 national universities (listed in chapter eight), 30 are need-aware institutions, six are need-blind and the other 64 offer no need-based aid for international students.

Need-aware institutions

Need-aware institutions and universities are those who assess an admission application aware of an applicant's/families' resources to meet the university financial obligations. These institutions have a certain amount of funding available to assist or aid international students. They offer need-based aid to those international applicants who have met the admission requirements but cannot meet the financial obligations of the university. These institutions appreciate the diversity and impact that international students bring to their campus and are, therefore, willing to financially aid them. It is important to stress, however, that these institutions have a limited amount of funding available for need-based international students.

Usually, students seeking need-based aid from need-aware institutions will be required to submit their financial statements (*CSS Profile* or equivalent) in conjunction with their admission application. Admissions decisions are made based on the applicant's admission criteria (grades, test scores, recommendations etc.) and the financial assistance required in the form of need-based aid. Offers of admission continue until the available funding is exhausted. International students will vary in their need-based requirement and their academic profiles. Evaluation of the applications and the financial profiles determine the best mix of international students, in the view of the university, within the limitations of their available financial aid. For example, if there is a student from a country X which has never sent a student to that specific institution and that student has a similar admission profile, but require more need-based aid than a student from country Y which has sent many students to that campus, it is possible that the university will offer admission to the student from country X, as they bring additional diversity to the campus. This is an example of just one criterion. There are many criteria that international admission officers must assess. Given the limited amount of funding, competitiveness within this need-based pool of international applicants is very high and is usually more competitive than the pool of applicants who do not require need-based aid. It is probable that some need-based aid students who meet the admission requirements at the university will not receive a place, due to their financial requirements. This is the reality of need-based aid for international students. Therefore, if you are able to meet the university financial obligations, it is good to confirm that with the university on the admissions application.

Duke University, a need-aware institution, explains it this way:

> "There are two applicant pools for foreign nationals: those not applying for financial aid (who will be considered for admission along with US citizens and lawful permanent residents), and those applying for financial aid (who will be considered in a separate process for a limited number of places in the entering class). Also, foreign citizens who do not apply for financial aid initially may not subsequently apply for financial aid during their time at Duke unless they become US citizens or lawful permanent residents". (Duke University 2009).

Once a positive admission decision is made for the student seeking need-based aid, institutions may require more information before awarding the final aid amount. If the student has been awarded other scholarships or funding from another source, students are required to notify the university of these awards. At almost every institution, aid is typically calculated by the formula:

Cost of Attendance – Expected Family Contribution (-other scholarships) =Award

or

COA – EFC (–other) = Award

Retaining these need-based aid awards usually requires students to maintain a certain *GPA* and remain *full-time* while at university. Some institutions may require students to re-apply each year. Students may also be required to work to offset some of the expenses. Each institution is different. NOTE: Many institutions will not allow second year students to apply for need-based aid. It is typically awarded in the first year or not at all.

Need-blind institutions

In contrast to need-aware institutions, there are six universities and colleges in the US that are need-blind for all students, including international applicants. They are Amherst College, Dartmouth College, Harvard University, Massachusetts Institute of Technology (MIT), Princeton University and Yale University. It is the mission of these institutions to admit the best and the brightest students from around the world. These universities make their admissions decisions without regard to any financial information from the students or parents. These institutions promise to meet the full financial need-based aid for all admitted students. Therefore, the cost of university should not be a factor for prospective students who believe they can earn a place at these universities. In some instances, these institutions will actually cost less than a university in the student's home country. However, admission at these institutions is extremely competitive.

Merit-based aid

Merit-based aid is university financial assistance awarded to a successful applicant based on a particular skill, talent or achievement.

The admission application process is very similar for students seeking merit-based aid as those seeking need-based aid. They will need to supply an application (either online through Common Application or via the university's own website) before the applicable deadline of each institution they are applying to, supplying the required admission documents. Some merit-based aid is awarded without a separate application (i.e. scholarships awarded via the admission application only). It is therefore important that a student's skill or talent is expressed within the admission application. Other merit-based aid could require a separate application, a portfolio, academic or other recommendations and possibly an essay or piece of writing. As a rule, merit-based aid awards are very competitive, but international students should still apply as they offer a global perspective that national students do not. Some institutions do not offer merit-based aid to international students, and some do not offer it to any student. The Ivy League, for example, does not offer merit based aid, only need-based aid. (University of Pennsylvania 2009).

Merit-based aid can come in many forms. It could be a tuition credit, a *full-ride award* or a specific monetary amount. Each package will be different. If a student receives various merit-based awards from different institutions, analyse them carefully and ask for clarification, if necessary. Universities that award a student aid will be interested to know if other universities have also offered aid packages. Alerting a university to the variances of the packages may prove to be worthwhile, financially speaking.

5. Full merit-based scholarships

There are numerous scholarships for undergraduate international students, but a few stand out as offering an excellent academic experience and covering all the costs of attendance. These scholarships are extremely competitive. The following scholarships welcome applications from international students and are listed in alphabetical order. Please note that details may change and each applicant should check the corresponding website for deadlines and the most up-to-date information.

Angier B. Duke Memorial Scholarship Program
Duke University, Durham, NC

"The A.B. Duke Scholarship Program provides more than a merit-based financial award. It offers support for the intellectually adventurous and curious. In addition to receiving financial awards covering full tuition, room and board, and all mandatory fees, A. B. Duke Scholars are encouraged to develop their own curricula and program-funded research projects". Each A.B. Duke Scholar receives a financial award and Duke will pay 100 percent of institutionally determined demonstrated need for U.S. citizens and non-citizens alike. "A.B. Duke Scholars excel academically, but they distinguish themselves in a variety of other ways. Chief among their unusual attributes is a self-motivated sense of discovery and a commitment to engage and meet the challenges faced by society at large: in the arts as well as sciences, in applied policy as well as theoretical economics, and many other areas". The AB Duke Scholarship awards full tuition, room and board, and all mandatory fees for four years (eight semesters). The number of awards varies. (The A.B. Duke Scholarship Program 2012).

The AU Emerging Global Leader Scholarship
American University, Washington D.C.

The AU Emerging Global Leader Scholarship promotes "access and opportunity while enhancing international diversity on American's campus. Preference is given to international students who have overcome various obstacles and challenges as well as those from diverse and underrepresented global and socioeconomic backgrounds. The most competitive applicants should have a minimum 3.8 GPA equivalent (or in the top 10% of graduating class), a demonstrated commitment to service and advancing the needs of people in their home country, excellent oral and written communication skills in English (minimum 90 TOEFL iBT) and demonstrated leadership, volunteerism and community service". This scholarship award includes full tuition, fees, room & board and is renewable with acceptable academic progress. Number of awards: one. (American University 2012).

International Special Scholarships
Grinnell College, Grinnell, IA

Grinnell offers a limited number of extremely competitive comprehensive scholarships that covers a majority of the costs associated with attending the College (including tuition, room and board, fees, health Insurance and books) that the student and their family are unable to cover. This funding is the result of gifts designated to support enrollment from specific world regions. There is no additional application form required, and all admitted Regular Decision students from the designated world regions are automatically considered for these awards. International Special Scholarships are designated for students from Africa, Eastern Europe, Eurasia, Latin America, Middle East, and Nepal as well as a native speaker of Russian (regardless of citizenship). These scholarships are renewable for three additional years of study. (Grinnell College 2012).

The Jefferson Scholarship
University of Virginia, Charlottesville, VA

The Jefferson Scholars Foundation's mission is "to attract to the University the most promising leaders, scholars, and citizens in the world and to give them sufficient financial support so that they are free to develop their talents and to use them for the good of the university community. The undergraduate Jefferson Scholarship began at the inception of Jefferson Scholars Foundation and has been attracting and cultivating undergraduate leaders since 1980. The program currently supports 110 Jefferson Scholars in residence at the University of Virginia".

In addition to the financial component (including tuition, fees, books, supplies, room, board and personal expenses) of the scholarship, there is an extensive enrichment programme which aims to support Jeff Scholars throughout their four years at UVa.

Each year the Foundation identifies finalists through several competitions: 54 regional competitions in the US, two international competitions and a separate competition open to other students, including international applicants to UVa. To be considered in the at-large and international screening processes, students must have applied to the University and returned their completed application to the Office of Admission by the regular decision deadline. We strongly recommend, however, that students submit their completed application to University of Virginia earlier in order to receive the fullest consideration. Additionally, at-large and international candidates must request that the Educational Testing Service forward their SAT results directly to the University.

Finalists are invited to Charlottesville (expenses fully paid) over the summer for a series of interviews, exams and conversations with attending faculty. Afterwards, the annual class of 27 Jeff Scholars are chosen. (Jefferson Scholars Foundation 2012).

John Montgomery Belk Scholarship
Davidson College, Davidson, NC

The John Montgomery Belk Scholarship programme is built around Davidson's belief that each "Belk Scholar possesses unique talents that should be recognised and nurtured. A candidate's academic record and recommendations must demonstrate purposeful engagement in the classroom, with student and civic organizations, on the athletic field or in the arts. While academic achievement is paramount, Belk Scholars also exhibit intellectual curiosity and a commitment to both their local and global communities".

Guidance counsellors, heads of school, or principals may nominate one candidate from each school by sending a recommendation, student's grades and school profile. Students must also submit their application for admissions early. The Davidson Admission Staff may also nominate candidates based on the strength of the students' applications for admission.

After phone interviews, finalists will visit Davidson for Belk Scholars Weekend (expenses fully paid) to participate in interviews conducted by selection committees composed of members of the Belk family, Davidson faculty, administrators, current and past Belk Scholars. (Davidson College 2012).

The Morehead-Cain Scholars Program
University of North Carolina, Chapel Hill, NC

Established in 1945 and inspired by the Rhodes Scholarship at the University of Oxford, the Morehead-Cain "provides an excellent undergraduate experience. The first programme of its kind in the US, the Morehead-Cain scholarship includes full financial support at the University of North Carolina at Chapel Hill. The scholarship covers full tuition, student fees, housing, meals, books and a laptop, supplies and miscellaneous expenses. Summer programmes place participants in valuable and worthwhile experiences in public

29

service, leadership and private enterprise with the overall goal to develop leaders".

Students apply to the University of North Carolina at Chapel Hill and are selected, or nominated by their school (country-specific) to apply to the Morehead-Cain. For students in countries where nominating schools have not been designated, the committee will select a few candidates for the scholarship. Applications for admission to UNC must be received in the Fall term of the final year of high school. In addition, students must submit a separate Morehead-Cain application. Finalists are invited to UNC (expenses fully paid) for interviews and the final selection. (The Morehead-Cain 2003–2012).

Presidential Scholarships
Boston College, Boston, MA

The Presidential Scholars Program "provides unusually accomplished students with opportunities to achieve their fullest potential. The selection committee are looking for students with outstanding academic records, who hold leadership roles in their school and who are committed to and have a demonstrated interest in community service".

There is no separate application process but to be considered students must apply by BC's early action admissions deadline. Finalists attend a final selection weekend in Boston (expenses fully paid). Candidates are interviewed by faculty and administrative staff and participate in other evaluative experiences, which all serve as the basis for the final choice of Presidential Scholars. Once admitted to BC as Presidential Scholars, students remain in the programme for their four years at BC as long as they maintain a 3.5 GPA and remain model citizens of the BC community. The scholarship award includes full tuition plus additional grants to cover all costs. (Boston College 2012).

The Presidential Scholarship Program
Villanova University, Villanova, PA

The Presidential Scholarship is awarded to 'students who have demonstrated academic achievement and active participation in their school and the broader civic community. Students must be nominated by the chief academic officer of their high school (principal, president or headmaster), guidance counsellor or an official school designee. They can also be nominated by a representative from a home school entity or non-profit educational organization dedicated to helping disadvantaged high school students with the college search process. Successful candidates are awarded this renewable scholarship, which covers tuition, general fee, room, board and books for eight consecutive semesters'.

Nominees will be expected to show evidence of superior academic performance as reflected by their high school course selection and *grade point average*, as well as a high SAT or ACT scores. The average combined SAT score (Critical Reading and Math) was 1450. Candidates will also be assessed in terms of leadership, civic engagement and ability to respond effectively to adversity, creativity and expertise in a specific field, with consideration given to a student's demonstrated financial need. Candidates will be required to complete a series of short essays to supplement the nomination form. A total of 28 Presidential Scholarships totalling nearly $1.5 million were offered to freshman candidates for the 2012-13 academic year. (Villanova University 2012).

The Robertson Scholars Program
Duke University, Durham, NC
University of North Carolina, Chapel Hill, NC

The Robertson Scholars Program was created in 2000 through a $24 million gift from Julian Robertson, a 1955 graduate of UNC and his wife Josie. "Inspired by their sons, one of whom graduated from Duke in 1998 and another who graduated from UNC-Chapel Hill in

2001, the Robertson's wanted to encourage further collaboration between the two universities".

Students apply to either Duke University or the University of North Carolina at Chapel Hill as normal. International applicants must be nominated or submit an application as directed by the specific country rules on the Robertson Scholar website. British students, for example, must be nominated by specified nominating schools or if warranted, their application for admission will be reviewed by the Robertson Committee. Other international students can submit an online application. The Program selects scholars "based not only on grades and traditional accomplishments, but also on other demonstrated personal attributes, including:

- strength of character to persevere and act on what they believe
- academic potential including critical thinking
- intellectual curiosity
- integrity, humility, courage, and compassion
- energy, initiative and the motivation necessary to accomplish great things"

Each year, the Robertson Scholars Program selects thirty-six new scholars, half attending Duke University and half attending the University of North Carolina at Chapel Hill. Robertson Scholars "have two dynamic intellectual homes at two superb universities Duke and UNC-Chapel Hill and full student privileges at both institutions. This includes access to courses; faculty and research opportunities; and arts, cultural, and sporting events. They hold a unique academic "dual citizenship" that offers them a wide variety of choices throughout their four years".

If selected, scholars attend the institution to which they were accepted with full tuition and living expenses paid. In their Spring semester of their second year, students transfer to the other institution. In years three and four, students can attend either institution. During their entire academic career, scholars have access to both campuses and the facilities. Students are expected to maintain a 3.0 GPA (2.8 GPA in first year) and be a full-time student. The Robertson Scholar programme expects participants to attend leadership programmes, dinners and be active in the university community. There is also a three part summer programme which is an integral part of the scholarship programme. (The Robertson Scholars Program 2005).

The Trustee Scholar Program
Boston University, Boston MA

Boston University's most prestigious merit-based award recognises "students who show outstanding academic and leadership abilities. Students from the United States and around the world are nominated by high school principals and headmasters. Those considered for the Trustee Scholarship typically rank in the top 5–10% of their class and demonstrate exceptional records of service and activity in their schools and communities. While the competition is especially rigorous, the benefits are considerable".

Applicants must be nominated by an educator at their home school and complete the essay form located on the website. An enrolment application (via Common Application) must be filled out and submitted according to the website deadline. Applications are reviewed by members of the faculty and staff of Boston University and selected trustee finalists will visit the BU campus for an interview weekend (expenses fully paid).

This scholarship is highly contested by students particularly active in community service. While essays for all of the top scholarships are important, the BU Trustee essay is particularly important. Faculty help choose the nominees and rely heavily on the essay submitted. Scholars live together on campus; participate in additional activities and network with the top academics at the University. A Trustee

Scholarship covers full undergraduate tuition plus the orientation and undergraduate student fees. If a student does not win one of the Trustee Scholarships, runners-up are often offered Presidential scholarships worth $20,000. (Boston University 2012).

What parents need to know

-by Alison M. Cooper

If your child is aiming for a place at a university in the USA there is a lot of work to be done – by them and by you. If they are serious then helping them to achieve their dream must be a carefully planned campaign. The key to success is to be open-minded, realistic and honest about what is possible and what is not, both in terms of the academic abilities of the student and the financial support structure of the family, before any applications are made.

Understanding a university's position on international students and financial support is vital before applying. Information available through the international undergraduate admissions pages on a university's website should explain their policies. This is where you can establish whether there is any financial support available from the university. This support can be in the form of need-based grants and scholarships based on the family's circumstances or merit-based support based on the student's academic record and, often, their extracurricular activities.

In addition to the emotional aspects of having a child at university in the USA, there will be a financial impact. Parents should decide at the beginning of the process whether they are willing to, and to what extent they are able to, financially help their child attend a US university. It is vital that parents consider and understand the financial implications of their child going to the US for university. Some families will be able to pay the full cost of a US college education, some will not. Financial support from the university may be the only way for some students to finance their education – whether this comes in the form of a merit-based scholarship or need-based financial aid. Your child needs to understand what is financially possible at the beginning as this will help determine which universities can be considered.

Need-based aid is a complex area and described thoroughly in Chapter 4. Each institution has its own policies and each family's circumstances are unique. Each aid package will be tailored to the individual student. Any need-based aid package will assume that parents (natural, adoptive and step) will contribute and that the student will contribute too, by working during the summer vacation and possibly during the academic year too. Merit-based scholarships are extremely competitive but this does not mean that they are impossible to achieve. You and your child need to have a full understanding of the financial value of a potential scholarship award.

Parents may find the range and depth of information about their financial situation that they have to provide quite intrusive when applying for need-based financial support. Some universities will allow parents to submit their financial information directly, but most will assume that this information is openly shared between parent and child. If you have never discussed your earnings, taxes, savings, investments, mortgage or the value of your house with your children, this process can come as a shock. However, this is a discussion that you will have to have before too long – in general terms at least – so that your child understands why they should not apply to certain institutions.

The situation is more complicated when parents are divorced, as most US universities will require the non-custodial parent to provide the same financial information. It should be noted that the information submitted by one parent is not available to the other. The non-custodial parent information is not available to the student either unless they choose to share it with them. Parents that have remarried should be aware that step-parents' finances are often taken into consideration too, particularly the step-parent that the child lives with.

In addition to the required forms certifying that they will financially support the student, parents or other sponsors will have to provide original documents providing proof that there are sufficient funds immediately available to cover the first year of costs. (Note: some institutions require proof that multiple years of expenses are immediately available). Parents need to plan ahead to arrange a bank letter or certified bank statements.

Even the most generous scholarships (*full-ride scholarships*) will need 'topping up' with the cost of flights, medical insurance (required at all US universities and by the visa rules) and other costs that arise as a result of being a student in another country. The opportunities for the student to earn money will be limited while they are at university due to US visa rules. Summer employment may not be possible if they have been awarded a scholarship which involves summer experiences.

Be realistic and honest with your child when they say they want to go the US. Help them to work out where they can apply and to understand what can be paid for (or cannot). Work with them to find the best possible scholarship opportunities and assist if more support from their high school is necessary. Finally, prepare yourself to let them go when all the effort has paid off. Most importantly, share their dream.

Editor note: Alison Cooper is the proud parent of a student attending a US institution on a full merit scholarship. Alison's life experiences include working as a shipbroker, molasses trader, student counsellor and international educator.

6. Other notable aid opportunities or programmes

Other notable opportunities for international students include the following unique scholarships and programmes. Many liberal arts colleges acknowledge the important impact that international student have on their campus and offer need-based or merit-based aid to international students. Please note that funding awards and amounts vary, details may change and each applicant should check the corresponding website for deadlines and the most up-to-date information.

Amherst College
Amherst, MA

Since the early 1900s, when the college began, Amherst has been committed to a strictly needs based financial aid policy. This generosity also extends to international students and over 80% of international students offered a place in the class of 2014 were offered a financial aid package. Competition for admission is strong with only 6.5% of international applicants offered admission for the class of 2014 and financial aid packages include a combination of scholarship and work. All students need to re-apply each year for financial aid. (Amherst College, 2012).

Bard College
Annandale-on-Hudson, NY
New Generation Scholarships

For students born abroad, or who are US born to immigrant parents, Bard College offers New Generation Scholarships. Students need to demonstrate a commitment to academic excellence and intellectual curiosity. Approximately 20 students per year are offered a New Generation Scholarship. Recipients need to maintain satisfactory academic standing and other requirements may be necessary as well. (Bard College 2012).

Colby College
Waterville, MA
The Colby-Oak Foundation International Scholarship

The Colby-Oak Foundation International Scholarship Program offers students who have suffered, or whose families have suffered political oppression, including political torture, the opportunity to qualify for a scholarship, if admitted to the college. Additionally the Oak Foundation awards two scholarships for students from Zimbabwe and with a preference for one or two scholarships for students from Denmark. Accepted Latin American students may qualify for a needs-based Neskowin Scholarship. (Colby College 2012).

The Cooper Union for the Advancement of Science and Art
New York City, NY

The extremely competitive Cooper Union, in Manhattan's East Village, provides extensive support for any admitted student, including international students. For the 2012-2013 academic school year, all admitted students receive the full-tuition scholarship, valued at $38,550. Cooper Union has received numerous awards and its programmes in architecture, engineering and fine arts are some of the best in the US. (Copper Union 2012).

Davis-United World College Scholars Program
Various locations

Launched in 2000 the Davis United World College Scholars Program is the world's largest, privately funded, international scholarship program. Since its founding it has provided scholarships to over

4,200 students from 146 countries, enabling them to study at over 90 different institutions across the US.

The Davis-UWC Program offers more than 350 full scholarships, and additional partial scholarships, each year, for graduates of United World Colleges who enrol in US colleges and universities.

To be eligible applicants need to have graduated from a United World Colleges (13 schools across Africa, Asia, Europe, Central and North America) and be accepted and enrol at an eligible US college or university. Once enrolled the Program provides financial support through need-based scholarships. (Davis-United World College Scholars Program, 2012).

Dickinson College
Carlisle, PA

All Dickinson College applicants, including international students will be considered for merit-based scholarships, in amounts from $10,000 to $20,000 per year. Scholarship awards are highly selective and require a separate application. Awards are based on a student's previous academic achievement, rigour of their high school curriculum, standardised test scores and demonstrated leadership in their school and community. (Dickinson College, 2012).

Emory University
Atlanta, GA
The Emory Scholars Program

The Emory College of Arts and Sciences offers full tuition scholarships based on academic merit to incoming first-year students as part of the Emory Scholars Program. Students can take advantage of special opportunities for research, study-abroad programmes and internships, as well as enjoy closer interactions with faculty. The Goizueta Scholarship offers similar opportunities, but is awarded by the Emory Goizueta School of Business.

"The Emory Scholars Program is designed to enrich your overall experience, broaden your intellectual horizons, strengthen your ethical sensibilities, and to deepen your personal growth". In addition to completing the Common Application and Emory supplement for admissions, applicants are required to supply a nomination from their school counsellor, an additional essay (different from the admissions essay) and a teacher recommendation. 350 semi-finalists are identified and then approximately 40 Finalists are invited to the Emory University campus (expenses fully paid) for a series of interviews, exams and conversations with faculty. (Emory University 2012).

Franklin & Marshall College
Lancaster, PA

Franklin & Marshall College offers need-based assistance to international students and will meet 100% of the demonstrated need of accepted international students. However as funding is limited the admissions process becomes more competitive the greater a student's financial need. Applicants need to submit the school's own international financial aid form. Currently IB students who score 30 points or more on their IB Diploma are granted 8 course credits, or the equivalent of one full year of credit towards a degree. Students who have taken individual Higher IB courses may also be eligible for credit. (Franklin & Marshall 2012).

Grinnell College
Grinnell, IA

In addition to their International Special Scholarships (see chapter five) Grinnell also offer academic merit scholarships to international students. Applicants do not need to demonstrate financial need for these scholarships and no additional application is required. For international students who do demonstrate financial need, grant assistance or student loans may be available. Loans for international students require a US citizen or US permanent resident as an approved co-signer. (Grinnell College 2012).

Jack Kent Cooke Undergraduate Transfer Scholarships
Various locations

The Foundation's Undergraduate Transfer Scholarships are awarded to the nation's top two-year, community college students with financial need to transfer to, and complete their Bachelor's degrees at a four-year college or university. The selection process for these awards is rigorous and highly competitive, with approximately 60 scholarships awarded each year. (Jack Kent Cooke Foundation 2008).

Lynn University
Boca Raton, FL
The Lynn 3.0 Program

The Lynn 3.0 Program allows students to complete their degree in three, rather than four years. Lynn 3.0 scholars will be required to participate in a May to June summer term, enrol in 18 credits per semester for their final two years of university and take 4 credits during the January term. Students can save an estimated $45,600 (tuition and fees, room and board, books, transportation and personal expenses) over the cost of a 4-year degree. Students are given priority course registration and do not incur additional charges for required summer courses and accelerated course loads.

Students with a minimum high school GPA of 3.0 and/or an SAT score of 1100 (in Math and Reading) are invited to enter the Lynn 3.0 Program. Students accepted into the 3.0 Program must formally re-commit each semester and must maintain satisfactory progress towards their degree. (Lynn University 2012).

Marquette University
Milwaukee, WI

"90% of the international students who applied for Fall 2010 admission received scholarships".

The Ignatius Scholarships
The Ignatius Scholarships are divided into two categories: academic achievement and service and leadership. Both scholarships are based on merit, not financial need. The Ignatius Scholarships for academic achievement range from $10,000 to $14,000 per year for up to four years. The Ignatius Scholarships for service and leadership are $8,000 per year for up to four years. Students will be considered for these awards based on their application for admission. However, a student who is interested in these scholarships should provide additional information which demonstrates their academic ability or service and leadership such as: school recommendation letters, academic rank, record of community service or a list of leadership activities. (Marquette University 2012).

Middlebury College
Middlebury, VT
Middlebury offers financial assistance based solely on established need and will meet 100% of the demonstrated need of all students they admit; international and US. There are no merit based awards offered. (Middlebury College 2012).

Oberlin College
Oberlin, OH

Oberlin offers financial assistance to international students in the form of grants, scholarships and on-campus employment. Admission is very competitive with typically less than 15% of international applications are admitted. However more than 80% of admitted international students receive financial aid and the average package covers approximately 75% of the cost of attendance.

For international applicants from Africa, Oberlin offers the Eduardo Mondlane Award. Japanese nationals accepted to Oberlin are eligible for the Ambassador Edwin O. Reischauer Scholarship. (Oberlin College 2012).

Oregon State University
Corvallis, OR
Provost International Scholarship

All international freshman and transfer students, with a GPA of 3.5 or higher, will be considered for Provost International Scholarships. Awards range from $6,000 - $9,000 per year for four years and no additional application materials are required. (Oregon State University 2012).

Saint John's College
Annapolis, MD and Santa Fe, NM

Offering a unique 'great books' curriculum that all students follow, no departments nor majors, St. John's College is a single college of two campuses; Annapolis and Santa Fe, each home to less than 500 students.

Each of the two campuses offer one fully funded needs-based scholarship to an incoming international student. Additionally institutional assistance awards can aid in covering up to 65% of the cost of tuition, room and board. International students are also eligible for low interest loans from the college. (St. Johns College 2012).

Smith College
Northampton, MA

Smith offers a limited number of awards based on merit rather than need. All applicants for admission are automatically considered; there is no special application. Students are selected by the Office of Admission and must maintain satisfactory academic progress in order to have their scholarships renewed annually. Merit aid is only offered at the time of admission.

STRIDE Scholarships

The STRIDE programme "offers students with outstanding academic and personal qualifications a close working relationship with a faculty member during their first two years at Smith. This scholarship of $15,000 per year for four years is awarded to approximately 50 students per year. In addition to the scholarship, students are also given an annual stipend of $2250 per year for two years that is linked to research with faculty members". (Smith College 2012).

Swarthmore College
Swarthmore, PA

Academically excellent international students who demonstrate financial need, and complete the aid application process may be offered scholarships from the following named funds, or other general funding sources. No separate application is required but financial need is a requirement for all scholarships. All scholarships are renewable each year, awards vary.

The Karim Abdel-Motaal '90 Egypt Scholarship gives preference firstly to students from Egypt, secondly to Arab or Arab American students and then to international students. Additional preference will be given to women candidates.

The Chloe and Raoul Glant Scholarship gives preference to a foreign or American student who demonstrates intellectual and personal integrity and a strong commitment to the public good.

The John W. '60 and Ann E. Harbeson Scholarship gives preference to a deserving international student, reflecting the donors' active involvement, careers and interests.

The Margaret Moore Scholarship gives preference to students of South Asian origin.

The Albert and Christine Nehamas Scholarship gives preference to students from Greece or other foreign countries.

The Mark L. Osterweil '94 Memorial Scholarship gives preference to American or foreign students whose studies of history are consistent with Mark Osterweil's interests in the economic, intellectual, political, and social relationships and connections between the United States and other countries, peoples, and cultures.

The Gehan Talwatte '87 and Keara Connolly '87 Endowed Scholarship gives preference to students from Sri Lanka, but other international students will also be considered.

The following scholarships are also awarded for academic merit and financial need, with a preference for international students.

The Vivian B. Allen Foundation

The Mark W. Crandall '80 International Scholarship

The Naomi Kies '62 Scholarship

The Hajime Mitarai Scholarship

The Martin S. and Katherine D. Quigley Scholarship

The Frances Reiner and Stephen Girard '41 Lax Scholarship

(Swarthmore College 2012).

Tulane University
New Orleans, LA
Global Scholarship

This award is specifically for international students with outstanding academic records. Applicants must complete both the Dean's Honors Scholarship application and the Global Scholars application which requires a project. Applicants must apply for admission to Tulane as early action and have a minimum of 650 on the Verbal portion of the SAT. The award is full-tuition, renewable for four years, (or five years for Architecture).

Dean's Honor Scholarships

To be eligible, applicants must submit their completed application for admission by the Early Action (non-binding) deadline and the Dean's Honor Scholarship application complete with Scholarship Recommendation. Typical scholarship recipients rank in the top 5 percent of their class, participate in a rigorous academic programme, have an outstanding record of extracurricular activities and high scores on the SAT or ACT. The award is full-tuition, renewable for four years, (or 5 years for Architecture). Number of awards: approximately 100 per year. (Tulane University 2012).

University of Portland
Portland, OR

International student scholarships are awarded to incoming and current international students based on academic merit and financial need. Undergraduate students may receive a maximum of $12,000 per year for tuition and fees. However, awards generally increase incrementally so first year students typically receive between $4,000-$6,000 increasing each year dependent on academic progress and financial need. A scholarship application is required. (University of Portland 2011).

46

Vassar College
Poughkeepsie, NY

Vassar College will meet 100% of the full demonstrated need of all admitted international and US students. For international students who demonstrated financial need and enrolled in the Class of 2012, the average scholarship was approximately $36,000 plus a Vassar student loan of $3,500, and eligibility for a campus job earning $1,720, for a total average financial aid award of approximately $41,000. (Vassar College 2012).

Wesleyan University
Middletown, CT

Wesleyan Freeman Asian Scholars Program

Students from 11 Asian countries (The People's Republic of China, Hong Kong, Indonesia, Japan, Malaysia, the Philippines, Singapore, South Korea, Taiwan, Thailand and Vietnam) who are not dual US citizens or permanent residents are eligible to apply for this full tuition scholarship. One national from each country is awarded a scholarship towards four years of Bachelor's degree study. Applicants need to take the SAT or ACT, as well as the TOEFL or IELTS. Additional information and essays are also required. Unsuccessful scholarship candidates will still be considered for admission if no financial aid is needed. (Wesleyan University 2012).

Williams College
Williamstown, MA

Williams will meet the full demonstrated financial need of every admitted student. The financial aid package is typically the difference between the complete COA of a Williams' education (tuition, room, board, books, fees and other expenses) and the amount the admitted student, and their family, is able to pay. (Williams College 2012).

7. Scenarios to reduce cost

For international students, it can be particularly important to find ways to reduce expenses given the cost of education on a US campus. In America, there are many ways to decrease your overall expenditure while still leaving the States with a four year undergraduate degree.

Transfer credit

Many international students attend high school a year longer than their US counterparts. International students may be able to apply this extra year of classes towards their university degree.

After being accepted to an institution, students should enquire at each university about applying their year 13 classes to their undergraduate degree. Many US universities have documents on their website showing the credit awarded for good IB scores. Credit for good A-Level or Abitur (and others) results are more subjective based on the varying degrees of high school's academic rigour.

For example, Duke University's website states:

Top tip

> "Entering students who have completed internationally recognized college-level examinations (the British "A" levels, the French Baccalaureate, the German Abitur or Swiss Maturite Certificate) with superior scores will receive international placement credit in essentially the same way that credit is awarded for AP exams." (Duke University 2012).

University credit for IB tends to be more standardised while credit for high A-level scores will vary widely among universities. Advanced Placement (AP) exams are also higher level exams offered in the US. A student applying to two different universities may be awarded varying amounts of credit for their IB or A-levels classes. Communicate this discrepancy in a polite and professional manner to the university that has awarded less credit. It is worth asking whether a university will match the credit transfer offer from the other institution. If not, ask them for their best and final offer, and make your admission decision. These questions should be directed to the Dean or Director of International Admissions at the university.

International students are also often able to test out of a foreign language requirement. For example, incoming Stanford University students can test out of their language requirement by achieving a certain score on the SAT II language exam. Students with excellent Spanish language skills who achieve 630 on the SAT II Spanish exam fulfil the required foreign language requirement. (Stanford University 2012).

An international student's IB example

"I was offered admission to my top two school choices, among others. As an IB diploma holder I was also offered credits towards my Bachelor's degree. I received scores of 6 on my Higher IB subjects; Economics, English and History. At the time I intended to study business, so I decided to make the best business decision I could and accepted my offer at the school that offered more credits; 18 credits (two, 3 credit courses for each IB Higher subjects) versus 12 credits (two, 3 credit courses for two of my IB Higher subjects). Additionally I placed out of the general education requirement to study a non-Western perspective course, having studied Asian history for IB, and could potentially place out of the foreign language requirement by taking a placement exam.

With the extra credits I earned from my IB Diploma I determined I could graduate in three years if I took extra credits in 4 semesters. As three year degrees are the norm in my home country this seemed like a good option. A full time student at my school needed to enrol in 12 credits (four, three credit classes) per semester, but 15 credits (five, three credit classes) was the norm. In one semester I took 21 credits (7 classes), which in hindsight I would not recommend and I took 18 credits (6 classes) for 3 semesters as well. In my final year I took 15 credits in the Fall and only 12 credits in my final semester. Although part of my courses in my final year was a credit bearing internship which involved working for 20 hours per week. I intentionally chose to increase my semester course load, rather than enrol in summer school, as there was no associated extra cost with enrolling in additional credits during the semester, but summer school carried a per credit charge. Additionally I wanted to work during the summer and have a break too!

Looking back I would advise other students attempting to do the same to choose their courses carefully and also to balance the work load. You can often take courses pass/fail which will still count towards your degree, and there is an amazing variety of fun classes like sports, film, dancing, food and beverage which you can take to balance the load. Ask for advice; every student at a US school will have an academic advisor, so share your goal with them. If they won't help or support you seek out someone else who will. By following my goal I was able to graduate in three years, with a double major, exactly 120 credits and saved a year's worth of tuition and expenses, over $40,000."

Community Colleges

For those students and families struggling to afford an education at a US university, a much less publicised way to significantly reduce cost is to attend a community college. We described the basics of a community college in chapter three, and admittedly, these schools do not typically have the breadth of programmes and activities available to students that four year universities offer. However, with a little creative thinking, students "can reduce the cost of their education by more than $40,000 over the two year period". (The College Board, 2008).

Here's how to achieve these savings. Once a target US university is identified, ask the admissions staff about transferring from a local community college. Each university has a list of area community colleges from which they accept transfer credit. More than likely, they will publish articulation agreements outlining the specific credits and courses from a community college that can be applied to a degree at the university. Students apply and attend the applicable community college for the first two years, earning the appropriate credits to transfer into the preferred four year university. Students who graduate from a community college also earn an *Associate's degree*.

Located near Washington D.C., Northern Virginia Community College (NOVA) offers off-campus housing, international support and a large variety of classes for incoming international students. When you meet the requirements of the NOVA *Guaranteed Admission Program,* credit can be transferred to various nearby universities including the University of Virginia's College of Arts & Sciences, the College of William & Mary and Virginia Tech. These are highly regarded institutions in the state of Virginia and are ranked in the top 100. (Northern Virginia Community College 2012).

It is less expensive to earn general education requirements at a community college than at a university. For example, four classes at NOVA are twelve credit hours, each of which costs approximately $332, for a total tuition of $3984. (Northern Virginia Community College 2012). After transferring, international students focus on upper-level major classes and, ultimately, earn the same undergraduate degree from the university as a four-year student does. True, the campus environment and 'scene' is not as extensive at a community college, but particularly in major urban centres, students can still feel a part of the nearby university by attending events, eating at local cafes and meeting university students.

Also consider the CUNY Borough of Manhattan Community College in New York for transfer credit to NYU or even Cornell. (CUNY Borough of Manhattan Community College 2012). In southern California, Santa Monica College graduates can apply credit to UCLA, the University of Southern California (USC) and many other California institutions. The City College of San Francisco is also a stepping stone to the University of California system or the California State university system. (City College of San Francisco 2012) In Miami, students earning credit at Miami-Dade College can apply to the University of Miami or even the University of Wisconsin-Madison (Miami-Dade College 2012). Most of the community colleges have offices dedicated to transfer students and will help you choose the correct classes. Of course, good grades will be essential and students will still need to apply and be accepted to the four year university as well.

There are other reasons to consider attending a community college. For students interested in interacting with faculty, the community college offers excellent access to members of faculty. Faculty at community college are rarely involved in research to the extent of their university colleagues. (United States Digest of Educational Statistics 1992). They are typically more accessible to students and can help as students adjust to life on campus. Secondly, acceptance rates for community college transfers are higher than for first year applicants. In the University of California system, preliminary data for 2010 shows that community college transfers are admitted at a rate of 80%. (University of California 2012).

International students interested in attending a community college prior to transferring to a four-year university will be particularly interested in the Jack Kent Cooke Undergraduate Transfer Scholarship described in chapter six.

Attend a less well-known US university

As discussed in chapter two, the benefits of a liberal arts education are numerous, particularly if a student is interested in pursuing a more specialised Master's degree. Most every institution in America offers a liberal arts education and the US degree is one of the most recognised in the world.

While the degree may be recognised outside of the US, the vast majority of US institutions are not well-known. As an international student, attending a lesser known university could mean paying lower tuition fees, living in a less expensive area of the US or being one of the few international students on campus. For example, Truman State University in Missouri is ranked no. 1 in the Midwest for regional colleges by the US News & World Report (2012) and has an enrolment of 5,675 with around 240 international students. (Truman State University 2012). Its *cost of attendance* (COA) per year for international students is $20,111. The COA at the University of Missouri is \$32,571 and at Washington University in St. Louis, the COA is \$63,205 for undergraduate international students.

The other advantages of a lesser known university could include increased opportunities to work on-campus as an international student given the relative low numbers, increased student support and a more relaxed atmosphere. Truman State is in Kirkland, Missouri, a small town in northeast Missouri. The overall cost of living in Kirkland is significantly cheaper than attending a larger university in a major metropolitan area.

Employment

Employment options for international students are available, but can be limited. In general, international students (F-1 and J-1 visa holders) are eligible to work on campus on a part-time basis, up to 20 hours per week. Second year students with F-1 and J-1 visas are eligible to work off campus only after obtaining specific employment authorisation from the international student office at their college or university. Permission to engage in off-campus employment must be obtained before beginning employment, even if it is for purposes of fulfilling an internship requirement. Students may be required to file US tax returns. Check with the international student office on campus for clarification and visa requirements.

Working will not typically cover the cost of tuition or housing, but it can be helpful in off-setting food costs and personal expenses. At the current US minimum wage set of \$7.25 per hour, a weekly allowance of over \$100 should satisfy most student expenses. International students can also gain significant cultural knowledge by working on-campus. (US Department of Labor 2011).

Ten other ways to save money on campus:

Top tips

- Buy clothes, computers and notebooks in the States. These items can be significantly cheaper there.

- Buy airline tickets early. Most school publish academic calendars in plenty of time so you can anticipate your flights to and from school. Some airlines offer student specials too.

- Use a credit card only in emergencies.

- Utilise websites like Craig's list or Freecycle for free or cheap furniture, school supplies and small appliances.

- Walk or bike to class or use free campus transportation.

- Look for local food & drink specials at area establishments.

- Buy used books and sell them after the term.

- Reuse a water bottle instead of buying bottled water.

- Use international student discount cards, like *I.S.I.C.*

- Participate...clubs, gyms and activities on campus are usually free.

8. Financial assistance available for international students from the top-ranked US universities

Below is an explanation of terms used in each university description. Universities included are the top nationally ranked universities for the 2012 academic year by the US News & World Report. (US News & World Report 2012).

Name:	Official name of the institution
Location:	City and state of the main campus
Web address	University home page
US News & World 2012:	The position of the school in the US News &World Report annual rankings.
QS Ranking 2012:	The position of the school in the QS World University Rankings.
Times Higher Ranking 2011-12:	The position of the school in Times Higher Education World University Rankings.
Admission Profile:	The admission profile for international students, see Glossary for definitions of need-aware and need-blind. The designation 'No need-based aid, n/a' means there is no need-based aid offered to international students, therefore the profile is not applicable.
Total Estimated cost: **(COA)**	The cost of attendance (COA) is for one academic year for international students. This is typically the amount of funding that an international student has to prove that they have; includes all costs once on-location.
Tuition element of costs:	Tuition fees for one academic year for an international student
Admission rate:	The published percentage of undergraduate applicants admitted as a percentage of undergraduate applications received
Admissions deadline:	The deadline for regular admission applications. See appendix for admissions deadlines and their meanings.

Scholarship application deadline:	The deadline for submitting a scholarship application. Application for admission to the university must also be submitted by this date if the scholarship deadline is earlier than the admissions deadline.
Common App®	Confirms whether online application can be made through commonapp.org .
Advanced credit:	Confirms whether IB and/or A Level results can be considered for advanced credits. Each university has specific rules on the use of advanced credits for exemption from particular courses/ modules or as replacement of a particular course/module that are part of general requirements, major or minor requirements.
International student financial support:	Summary of university policy on availability of funding for international students.
Financial Documentation required:	Information on financial documents that is required for admission and when they need to be submitted.
Merit Scholarships:	Summary of scholarships offered to international students, if applicable.
Class Profile:	The average scores of the entering class, as published by the university. 25/75 percentile means that 25% of the class scored at or below the lower score listed and 75% of the class scored at or below the higher score listed. SAT section scores are out of 800 points, for 2400 total. ACT maximum is 36.

NOTE: All of the deadlines and dates listed here are correct at the time of publishing. While we strive to provide accurate information, universities change their information regularly. Please consult the individual websites to confirm the deadlines for all application materials. We cannot be held responsible for changes in information. Institutions are presented in alphabetical order.

Name:	**American University**
Location:	**Washington, D.C.**
Website:	**www.american.edu**
US News & World 2012:	**82 (tied)**
QS Ranking 2012:	**601+**
Times Higher Ranking 2011-12:	**not listed**
Admission Profile:	No need-based aid, n/a
Cost of attendance:	$55,289 (2012-2013)
Tuition element of cost:	$39,982
Admission rate:	41%
Admission deadline:	January 15
Scholarship deadline:	January 15
Common App®:	Yes
Advanced credit:	Higher IB

International student financial support:

AU does not provide need-based financial aid to international students. International students are eligible for merit awards, which are partial scholarships and very competitive.

Financial Documentation required

AU Certification of Finances for International Students form submitted as part of application for admission.

Merit Scholarships

Recipients of these merit scholarships demonstrate a combination of outstanding academic achievement, excellent communication skills in English, leadership, volunteerism, and community service. No additional application is required but to be considered students must have submitted proof that they have the funds to study at AU as part of their application for admission.

Award: $6000 to $32,000, renewable for all four years of study based on successful continued academic performance. The number of awards varies.

The AU Emerging Global Leader Scholarship

See chapter five

Freshman Profile Class of 2015

SAT/ACT scores are NOT reviewed for students from high-schools outside the USA.

Name:	**Auburn University**
Location:	**Auburn, Alabama**
Website:	**www.auburn.edu**
US News & World 2012:	**82 (tied)**
QS Ranking 2012:	**601+**
THE Ranking 2011-12:	**351-400**
Admission Profile:	No need-based aid, n/a
Cost of attendance:	$42,292 (2012-2013)
Tuition element of cost:	$25,190
Admission rate:	70%
Admission deadline:	February 1
	December 1 for merit scholarship consideration
Scholarship deadline:	December 1
Common App®:	No
Advanced credit:	Higher IB

International student financial support:
Auburn University does not provide need-based financial aid to international students. AU does offer a limited number of scholarships to international students who have excelled academically.

Financial Documentation required
Affidavit Of Financial Support For International Student Undergraduate Admission To Auburn University submitted as part of application process.

Academic Scholarships
Academic scholarships are awarded competitively to non-US residents based on SAT/ACT scores and high-school performance. The minimum test scores do not guarantee a scholarship but all eligible applications will be considered provided that the complete admission application is submitted by December 1. There is not separate application.

Presidential Scholarship
Students must achieve 34-36 ACT or 1490-1600 SAT score and have a minimum 3.5 high school GPA for consideration.
Award: $15,000 per year, a $1,000 technology stipend the first fall semester, and an invitation to participate in the University Honours College, renewable for a total of four years. The number of awards vary.

Heritage Scholarship
Students must achieve 31-33 ACT or 1360-1480 SAT score and have a minimum 3.5 high school GPA for consideration. Award: $10,000 per year, renewable for a total of four years. The number of awards varies.

Charter Scholarship
Students must achieve 29-30 ACT or 1290-1350 SAT score and have a minimum 3.5 high school GPA for consideration.
Award: $5,000 per year, renewable for up to four years
The number of awards varies.

Elite Scholarships
The University Scholarship Committee invites a select group of eligible incoming non-US resident freshmen to apply for AU's most prestigious scholarships. Students invited to apply in December are those with a minimum 34 ACT or 1490 SAT score and a 3.5 high school GPA by the December 1 Freshman Scholarship priority deadline. Following a January application deadline, finalists are invited to campus in February to interview.
Award: between $10,000 and $30,000 over four years ($2,500 to $7,500 per year).
Number of awards: up to 14

Auburn Spirit Foundation Scholarship
Incoming non-US resident freshmen who meet the December 1 Freshman Scholarship priority deadline receive automatic consideration. Auburn Spirit Foundation Scholarships are awarded among students with a minimum 26 ACT or 1170 SAT score and a 3.5 high school GPA who have not already been recognized by the Office of University Scholarships with a scholarship of equal or greater value. Additional consideration is given to first generation college students.
Award: $6,000 over four years ($1,500 per year). The number of awards varies.

Freshman Profile Class of 2015
Average SAT 1233
Average ACT 27

Name:	Baylor University
Location:	Waco, Texas
Website:	www.baylor.edu
US News & World 2012:	75 (tied)
QS Ranking 2012:	601+
THE Ranking 2011-12:	not listed
Admission Profile:	No need-based aid, n/a
Cost of attendance:	$48,002 (2012-2013)
Tuition element of cost:	$30,586
Admission rate:	39%
Admission deadline:	February 1 but November 1 recommended for international students
Scholarship deadline:	February 1
Common App®:	No
Advanced credit:	Higher and Subsidiary IB

International student financial support:

Baylor does not provide need-based financial aid to international students. Applicants are automatically considered for various freshmen merit scholarships. In addition there some on-campus jobs available to international students whose immigration status allows them to work.

Financial Documentation required

Baylor's Confirmation of Financial Resources submitted after admission.

Freshmen Academic Scholarships

At the time of admission, all international freshmen are considered for one of the following awards based on their combined SAT Critical Reading and Math scores. Renewal is contingent on recipients maintaining full-time enrolment and a cumulative minimum 3.0 GPA.

President's Gold Scholarship

Award: $42,000-$68,000 divided over 8 undergraduate semesters.

Provost's Gold Scholarship

Award: $34,000-$50,000 divided over 8 undergraduate semesters.

Deans' Gold Scholarship

Award: $12,000-$44,000 divided over 8 undergraduate semesters.

Freshman Profile Class of 2015

Median SAT range 1140-1320

Median ACT range 24-29

Name:	Binghamton University
Location:	Binghamton, New York
Website:	www.binghamton.edu
US News & World 2012:	90 (tied)
QS Ranking 2012:	601+
THE Ranking 2011-12:	301-350
Admission Profile:	No need-based aid, n/a
Cost of attendance:	$31,397 (2012-2013)
Tuition element of cost:	$14,718
Admission rate:	33%
Admission deadline:	February 15
Scholarship deadline:	n/a
Common App®:	Yes
Advanced credit:	Higher IB

International student financial support:
Binghamton does not offer need-based or merit-based aid to international students.
Financial Documentation required
International Student Financial Statement submitted after admission.
Freshman Profile Class of 2015
SAT mid-range
Math: 610-710
Critical Reading: 580-680
Writing: 570-670
Average ACT score Mid-Range: 26-30

Name:	Boston College
Location:	Boston, Massachusetts
Website:	www.bc.edu
US News & World 2012:	31 (tied)
QS Ranking 2012:	329
THE Ranking 2011-12:	195
Admission Profile:	No need-based aid, n/a
Cost of attendance:	$65,552 (2012-2013)
Tuition element of cost:	$43,140
Admission rate:	28%
Admission deadline:	January 1
	November 1 for Presidential Scholarship consideration
Scholarship deadline:	November 1
Common App®:	Yes
Advanced credit:	Higher IB and A Level

International student financial support:
Boston College does not provide need-based financial aid to international students, but there is merit-based aid available. International applicants are eligible to receive a Presidential Scholarship. All international students must submit a confidential declaration of finances form to verify funding for visa purposes.

Financial Documentation required
BC's Confidential Declaration of Finances Form submitted after admission.

Presidential Scholarships
See chapter five

Freshman Profile Class of 2015
SAT Average: (Critical Reading, Math, Writing) 2014
Mid 50% SAT Range 1920-2135

Name:	Boston University
Location:	Boston, Massachusetts
Website:	www.bu.edu
US News & World 2012:	53 (tied)
QS Ranking 2012:	64
THE Ranking 2011-12:	54
Admission Profile:	Need-aware
Cost of attendance:	$63,126 (2012-2013)
Tuition element of cost:	$42,400
Admission rate:	58%
Admission deadline:	January 1
	December 1 for Trustee and Presidential Scholarship
Scholarship deadline:	December 1
Common App®:	Yes
Advanced credit:	Higher IB
	A and AS Level

International student financial support:
BU does not provide need-based financial aid to international students. There are two merit-based scholarships open to international students, one of which requires a separate application.

Financial Documentation required
BU's Confidential Statement for Financing Studies submitted with application for admission.

Trustee Scholarship
See chapter five

Presidential Scholarships
BU's Board of Admissions awards the Presidential Scholarship to freshmen who demonstrate exceptional academic achievement and who demonstrate excellence beyond the classroom and leadership. No additional essays or application forms are required. The award process is very competitive and to be eligible for consideration students must submit their completed application by December 1. Award: up to $20,000 of tuition, renewable for four years. Number of awards: approximately 5% of freshman class.

Freshman Profile Class of 2015
SAT Composite Average: 2005. ACT Average: 29

Name:	Brandeis University
Location:	Waltham, Massachusetts
Website:	www.brandeis.edu
US News & World 2012:	31 (tied)
QS Ranking 2012:	332
THE Ranking 2011-12:	150
Admission Profile:	Need-aware
Cost of attendance:	$60,800 (2012-2013)
Tuition element of cost:	$42,682
Admission rate:	40%
Admission deadline:	January 15
Scholarship deadline:	January 15
Common App®:	Yes
Advanced credit:	Higher IB

International student financial support:
Brandeis University requires all international applicants to provide financial information in conjunction with the application for admission. Brandeis offers a competitive programme of scholarship and financial aid for international students. Giving more than $1 million in scholarships to international students each year, Brandeis will meet 100% of demonstrated financial need for admitted international students. To be considered for these scholarships, international students must submit the CSS Profile and supporting financial documents at the time of application.

International students who are not awarded financial aid for their first year will not be able to receive financial aid in future years. It is imperative that applicants who will need financial aid during college apply for financial aid when they apply for admission. All scholarships are awarded for four years of study at Brandeis, beginning with the semester for which the student is admitted.

Financial documents provide information that will place international applicants into one of two categories prior to the admission decision. Students who do not require aid are placed into the same pool with all other incoming freshman. As international aid funds are limited, all students requiring aid will be in a more competitive category.

Financial Documentation required
Submit the following as part of admissions application:
CSS Profile if applying for need-based aid
International Student Certification of Finances if no need-based aid required.

Wien International Scholarship Program
This need-based scholarship meets the full demonstrated financial need of each recipient and includes funds for one round-trip air ticket each year between the

United States and the student's home country. Wien Scholarships are awarded to exceptionally accomplished international applicants who demonstrate strong academic achievement as well as significant extracurricular or community involvement.

Alumni and Friends Scholarships

Alumni and Friends Scholarships combine scholarship, university employment and loan to meet the demonstrated financial needs of admitted international students.

Freshman Profile Class of 2016

SAT (25/75 percentile) 1280-1420   Critical reading (25/75) 600-710

Math (25/75) 630-740

Name:	**Brigham Young University**
Location:	**Provo, Utah**
Website:	**www.byu.edu**
US News & World 2012:	**71 (tied)**
QS Ranking 2012:	**601+**
THE Ranking 2011-12:	**not listed**
Admission Profile:	No need-based aid, n/a
Cost of attendance:	$23,800 (2012-2013)
Tuition element of cost:	$9,420
Admission rate:	64%
Admission deadline:	February 1
Scholarship deadline:	February 1
Common App®:	No
Advanced credit:	Higher and Subsidiary IB

International student financial support:
BYU does not provide need-based financial aid to international students. International students can apply for merit/academic scholarships.

Financial Documentation required
BYU's International Student Affidavit of Support submitted after admission.

Academic Scholarships
BYU scholarship funds are provided through tithes of The Church of Jesus Christ of Latter-Day Saints, along with offerings from friends of the university. Scholarships are awarded in order to encourage continued commitment to spiritual and intellectual growth. Scholarship awards are primarily based on academic achievement and composite ACT/SAT scores. There is a specific online application process and there are three versions. The comprehensive version does not apply to international students. International students should fill out the enhanced or basic version as there is no need-based financial aid for international students.

Enhanced: students considered for most scholarships that are awarded through the Financial Aid Office, except those with a need-based component. This version requires three essays.

Basic: By completing the Basic Application, students will only be considered for academic scholarships. Most BYU scholarships are awarded for two semesters only and students must re-apply every year. About half of the first year students with a one-year scholarship qualify for a scholarship in the second year.

Award: up to $5,000. The number of awards varies.

Freshman Profile Class of 2015
Average Composite ACT 28

Name:	**Brown University**
Location:	**Providence, Rhode Island**
Website:	**www.brown.edu**
US News & World 2012:	**15 (tied)**
QS Ranking 2012:	**42**
THE Ranking 2011-12:	**49**
Admission Profile:	Need-aware
Cost of attendance:	$58,140 (2012-2013)
Tuition element of cost:	$43,758
Admission rate:	9%
Admission deadline:	January 2
Scholarship deadline:	February 1
Common App®:	Yes
Advanced credit:	Higher IB and A Level

International student financial support:
Brown does not award academic, athletic or merit scholarships.
Brown considers international applicants on a need-aware basis and will take into account their financial need in making admission decisions. However, for those foreign applicants that are admitted, Brown will meet 100% of their demonstrated financial need. Brown financial assistance will be in the form of tuition waiver, paid accommodation or other credits. Financial aid covers books and some personal expenses, but does not cover vacation and summer expenses. Foreign citizens who do not receive financial aid at the time of admission will not be considered for aid at a later date. Foreign citizens must apply for financial aid at the time of application if they have reason to believe they will need assistance at any point during their time at Brown.

Financial Documentation required
If applying for financial support submit the CSS Profile and Noncustodial parent profile by November 1.

Freshman Profile Class of 2015
The middle 50 percent of admitted students scored between 1350 and 1510 on the Math and Critical Reading portions of the SAT.
The middle 50 percent of admitted students scored between 30 and 34 on the ACT.

Name:	California Institute of Technology
Location:	Pasadena, California
Website:	www.caltech.edu
US News & World 2012:	5 (tied)
QS Ranking 2012:	10
THE Ranking 2011-12:	1
Admission Profile:	Need-aware
Cost of attendance:	$56,382 (2012-2013)
Tuition element of cost:	$38,085
Admission rate:	13%
Admission deadline:	January 3
Scholarship deadline:	January 15
Common App®:	Yes
Advanced credit:	Caltech accepts the IGCSE, O, AS and A Level, and IB credit to satisfy course requirements.

International student financial support:

Caltech has financial aid available for international freshman candidates. However, admission is not need-blind for these applicants, as it is for United States citizens and permanent residents. Admission for international students seeking financial aid is very competitive. International undergraduate applicants who do not apply for financial aid by published deadlines in conjunction with their application for admission, or who are denied aid for their first year at Caltech, are not eligible for need-based financial aid for any other academic period while they are undergraduates at the Institute (with the exception of citizens of Canada and Mexico). Those with financial aid offers will be eligible to apply for assistance in subsequent years. All eligible students must reapply for aid each year. Merit scholarships (named awards) are available at Caltech for international students. At the time of printing, after numerous requests, no further information is available.

Financial Documentation required

Caltech International Freshman Financial Aid Statement of Intent and, if applying for aid, CSS Profile submitted as part of application for admission.

Freshman Profile Class of 2015

SAT mid-50%: 2200-2340

ACT mid-50% (composite): 33–35

Name:	Carnegie Mellon University
Location:	Pittsburgh, Pennsylvania
Website:	www.cmu.edu
US News & World 2012:	23 (tied)
QS Ranking 2012:	49
THE Ranking 2011-12:	21
Admission Profile:	No need-based aid, n/a
Cost of attendance:	$63,510 (2012-2013)
Tuition element of cost:	$44,880
Admission rate:	21%
Admission deadline:	January 1
Scholarship deadline:	n/a
Common App®:	Yes
Advanced credit:	Higher IB and A Level

International student financial support:
CMU does not provide need-based or merit-based financial aid to international students. International students must assume the total cost of a Carnegie Mellon education. Financial aid is not available to international undergraduates and applicants must complete CMU's online preliminary application before submitting their application through Common App®. This form is used to verify the student's ability to pay for their CMU educationand without it an application will not be processed.

Financial Documentation required
international students must submit CMU Pre-Application form verifying finances.

Freshman Profile Class of 2015

Middle 50% range	Mean ACT scores:
SAT-CR 660-750	ACT English: 31
SAT-M 670-770	ACT Math: 31
SAT-WR 680-760	ACT Comp: 31

Name:	**Case Western Reserve**
Location:	**Cleveland, Ohio**
Website:	**www.case.edu**
US News & World 2012:	**38 (tied)**
QS Ranking 2012:	**164**
THE Ranking 2011-12:	**93**
Admission Profile:	Need-aware
Cost of attendance:	$56,491 (2012-2013)
Tuition element of cost:	$40,120
Admission rate:	51%
Admission deadline:	January 15
Scholarship deadline:	January 15
Common App®:	Yes
Advanced credit:	IB and A Level

International student financial support:
Case Western offers some limited need-based financial aid and merit-based scholarships requiring an additional application, audition or portfolio to international students.

Financial Documentation required
CSS Profile if applying for need-based aid.

Andrew and Eleanor Squire Scholarship
This four-year full-tuition scholarship was originally established by Case Western Reserve University trustee Andrew Squire and his wife Eleanor to encourage students to learn about the outdoors. Applicants must complete online application form. Number of awards: two

A.W. Smith Innovation Scholarship
The A.W. Smith Innovation Scholarship awards full tuition to students with the potential for significant innovation in the fields of engineering or science. Apply online. Number of awards: two

Case Western Reserve University Leadership Scholarships
These scholarships are awarded to students who display outstanding leadership in their academic and extracurricular pursuits. Apply online.
Awards: between $2,500 to $10,000. The number of awards varies.

Alexander A. Treuhaft Memorial Scholarship
This scholarship for four years of tuition is offered to the outstanding first-year applicants in science and engineering. Apply online. Number of awards: varies

Milton A. and Roslyn Z. Wolf Scholarship
This full tuition scholarship is awarded based first upon character or a student's demonstrated potential to be a leader and "make a difference in the world" and

secondly upon their academic performance, intellect and accomplishments. Apply online. Number of awards: varies

Performing Arts Scholarships

Full tuition scholarships are awarded to students who exhibit excellence in the performing arts and will major in music, theatre or dance. Scholarships are awarded based on an audition. Contact the individual departments to arrange an audition.

Creative Achievement Awards

Scholarships are awarded to students who exhibit excellence in music or visual arts but will not major in these subject areas. Scholarships are awarded based on an audition or portfolio review. Contact the individual departments to arrange for an audition.

Freshman Profile Class of 2015

Test Scores of Middle 50th Percentile

SAT Critical Reading 600-690

SAT Math 650-750

SAT Writing 590-690

ACT 28-32

Name:	**Clark University**
Location:	**Worcester, Massachusetts**
Website:	**www.clarku.edu**
US News & World 2012:	**94 (tied)**
QS Ranking 2012:	**601+**
THE Ranking 2011-12:	**not listed**
Admission Profile:	Need-aware
Cost of attendance:	$50,681 (2012-2013)
Tuition element of cost:	$38,100
Admission rate:	69%
Admission deadline:	January 15
Scholarship deadline:	January 15
Common App®:	Yes
Advanced credit:	IB Diploma score of 36 or more, with 5 on each of 6 exams, will receive one full year of credit

International student financial support:
Clark's admission process for international students is need-aware. International applicants are eligible for both need-based and merit-based assistance but funds are limited. Awards are made during the admission process and students not receiving an award at the time of admission will not be eligible to receive one in future years. Clark expects students and their families to contribute to the cost of education and need-based funds are reserved for students who show that they are clearly able to fund at least part of their education.

Financial Documentation required
CSS Profile for need-based aid to be submitted by January 15. Non-custodial Parent Profile if relevant.

LEEP Scholars Program
Launched in 2012 the LEEP (Liberal Education and Effective Practice) Scholars programme is open to international students. Candidates will be ambitious students with strong high school records that make them top applicants academically and demonstrate drive, creativity and the passion to tackle complex challenges. Students will be required to complete a LEEP Project on a topic of their choice. Qualified LEEP Scholars who meet the eligibility requirements for the Accelerated B.A./Master's Degree Program also have the opportunity to earn both a Bachelor's and Master's degree in five years with the fifth year tuition-free. Finalists will be chosen based the strength of their applications for admission and on the quality of their LEEP essays. Clark will invite 10 to 15 finalists to participate in an on-campus interview in March. Award includes full tuition, room and board for four years, a stipend to support the LEEP Project. Number of awards: five per year

Global Scholars Program Scholarship
Based on merit, this scholarship builds on Clark University's long-standing commitment to providing a challenging education with a global focus. The Global Scholars Program (GSP) is a special programme for incoming international students who have demonstrated outstanding leadership in their home communities before attending Clark. High school academic records must also be strong. Recipients are required to perform community service each year. Award: no less than $15,000 per year, for up to four years, renewable provided minimum 3.0 GPA Number of awards: varies

Freshman Profile Class of 2015
SAT/ACT optional
25/75 Percentile results
SAT Critical Reading 540 660
SAT Math 530 640
SAT Writing 550 650
SAT Essay 24 30
ACT Composite 25 31
ACT Math 23 29
ACT English 25 31
ACT Writing 8 9

Name:	**Clemson University**
Location:	**Clemson, South Carolina**
Website:	**www.clemson.edu**
US News & World 2012:	**68 (tied)**
QS Ranking 2012:	**601+**
THE Ranking 2011-12:	**351-400**
Admission Profile:	No need-based aid, n/a
Cost of attendance:	$43,148 (2011-2912)
Tuition element of cost:	$29,085
Admission rate:	60%
Admission deadline:	May 1
Scholarship deadline:	n/a
Common App®:	No
Advanced credit:	Higher IB

International student financial support:
Clemson does not provide any financial aid to international students. Verification that sufficient funds are available is an integral part of the admission process.

Financial Documentation required
Clemson's Financial Certification Form submitted with application.

Freshman Profile Class of 2015
SAT Average 1230
SAT Range 1140-1330
ACT middle 50 percent score range is 26 to 30 for the composite

Name:	College of William & Mary
Location:	Williamsburg, Virginia
Website:	www.wm.edu
US News & World 2012:	33 (tied)
QS Ranking 2012:	501-550
THE Ranking 2011-12:	146
Admission Profile:	Need-aware
Cost of attendance:	$51,848 (2012-2013)
Tuition element of cost:	$38,118
Admission rate:	35%
Admission deadline:	January 1
Scholarship deadline:	January 1
Common App®:	Yes
Advanced credit:	Higher level IB

International student financial support:
William & Mary does not provide need-based financial aid to international students. There are merit scholarships that may consider international students.

Financial Documentation required
W&M's Certification of Financial Support for International Students submitted as part of application for admission.

William & Mary Scholars
William and Mary Scholar Awards are presented each year to a small, select group of students who have overcome unusual adversity and/or would add to the diversity of the campus community. All applicants are considered for the award and no separate application is needed.
Award: varies on personal circumstance, up to full tuition
The number of awards varies.

James Monroe Scholars
The James Monroe Scholars Program is offered each year to the top 10-15% of all admitted students to the College of William and Mary. All first-year applicants are considered for this programme and no separate application is needed. High achieving freshmen may be offered the opportunity to become a Monroe Scholar in their sophomore year. Award: $3000 summer research stipend and added benefits, such as preferred housing, preferential course registration and advising.
The number of awards varies.

The Murray Scholars Program
The Murray Scholars Program is William & Mary's most selective scholarship.
Finalists typically rank in the top 1% of their class, score a 1500 and higher on the SAT Critical Reading plus Math (ACT equivalent: 34 or higher) and take the most demanding curriculum available to them. While some of the variables that

influence Murray Scholars designations are quantitative, others are more subjective. These include students' application essays, extracurricular involvements, leadership, letters of recommendation, and evidence of intellectual engagement. Award: Full, in-state tuition, general fees and room and board annually, equivalent amount for out-of-state students. Number of awards: four

Clark-Campbell Scholarship

This one-time scholarship is awarded to an international undergraduate student who has distinguished him/herself in academics and service to the W&M community. Award: $3,000 to rising second year international student. Number of awards: one

Jack Wolf Scholarship

This one-time scholarship is awarded to an international undergraduate student who has distinguished him/herself in academics, leadership, and service to the W&M community. Award: maximum of $3,500. Number of awards: one

Freshman Profile Class of 2015

25/75th Percentile
SAT Critical Reading 620 730
SAT Math 620 720
SAT Writing 620 720
ACT Composite 28 32
ACT Math 27 32
ACT English 28 34

Name:	**Colorado School of Mines**
Location:	**Golden, Colorado**
Website:	**www.mines.edu**
US News & World 2012:	**75 (tied)**
QS Ranking 2012:	**not listed**
THE Ranking 2011-12:	**not listed**
Admission Profile:	No need-based aid, n/a
Cost of attendance:	$51,784 (2012-2013)
Tuition element of cost:	$28,620
Admission rate:	46%
Admission deadline:	April 1
Scholarship deadline:	n/a
Common App®:	Yes
Advanced credit:	Higher IB

International student financial support:
The Colorado School of Mines does not provide any financial aid to international students.

Financial Documentation required
Certification of Finances for International Students form submitted as part of application for admission.

Freshman Profile Class of 2015
Test Scores -- 25th / 75th Percentile
SAT Critical Reading: 570 / 675
SAT Math: 630 / 710

Name:	**Columbia University**
Location:	**New York, New York**
Website:	**www.columbia.edu**
US News & World 2012:	**4**
QS Ranking 2012:	**11**
THE Ranking 2011-12:	**12**
Admission Profile:	Need-aware
Cost of attendance:	$61,740 (2011-2012)
Tuition element of cost:	$45,028
Admission rate:	7%
Admission deadline:	January 1
Scholarship deadline:	March 1
Common App®:	Yes
Advanced credit:	Higher IB and A Level

International student financial support:

As a member of the Ivy League, there are no academic, athletic or talent-based institutional scholarships at Columbia and all institutional financial aid is need-based. Columbia meets 100% of the demonstrated financial need for all students, including international students, for all four years of study. Eligibility for need-based financial aid is determined by many factors, including the family's income, assets, family size and number of children in college. Students and their families are expected to contribute to the cost of attending Columbia to the extent that they are able.

Admission is not need-blind for international students. Although financial aid is available for foreign students, candidates should be aware that their applications are read in a more selective process than are other candidates. International students who do not apply for financial aid at the time of applying for admission are not able to apply at a later stage.

Financial Documentation required

If applying for financial aid submit the CSS and, if applicable, the non-custodial parent profile by March 1.

Freshman Profile Class of 2015

The middle 50% of admitted students scored between 2150 and 2320 on the Math, Critical Reading and Writing sections of the SAT. The middle 50% of admitted students scored between 32 and 35 on the ACT.

Name:	**Cornell University**
Location:	**Ithaca, New York**
Website:	**www.cornell.edu**
US News & World 2012:	**15 (tied)**
QS Ranking 2012:	**14**
THE Ranking 2011-12:	**20**
Admission Profile:	Need-aware
Cost of attendance:	$59,591 (2012-2013)
Tuition element of cost:	$43,413
Admission rate:	18%
Admission deadline:	January 2
Scholarship deadline:	January 2
Common App®:	Yes
Advanced credit:	Higher IB and A Level

International student financial support:

Cornell has a need-aware international admissions policy. Cornell awards all financial aid on the basis of demonstrated financial need. Cornell is pleased to be able to provide financial aid to a limited number of students who are citizens of countries other than the United States. No merit aid or athletic scholarships are awarded at Cornell.

Financial Documentation required

If applying for financial aid, submit the CSS Profile, Cornell International Financial Aid Application and, if appropriate, the International Student Financial Aid Application for non-custodial parent.

Freshman Profile Class of 2015

Average

SAT I Critical Reading 678

SAT I Math 715

SAT I Total 1,393

ACT Composite 31

Name:	**Dartmouth College**
Location:	**Hanover, New Hampshire**
Website:	**www.dartmouth.edu**
US News & World 2012:	**11**
QS Ranking 2012:	**113**
THE Ranking 2011-12:	**90**
Admission Profile:	Need-blind
Cost of attendance:	$61,683 (2012-2013)
Tuition element of cost:	$43,782
Admission rate:	10%
Admission deadline:	January 1
Scholarship deadline:	n/a
Common App®:	Yes
Advanced credit:	Higher IB and A Level

International student financial support:

The financial aid policies for foreign citizens are exactly the same as those for U.S. citizens. All aid is need-based, and admissions decisions are made without regard to whether an applicant has applied for financial assistance. Dartmouth awards scholarships and financial aid on the basis of a student's ability to afford the costs of a Dartmouth education. As a member of the Ivy League, Dartmouth does not award academic, athletic or merit scholarships. Dartmouth guarantees to meet 100% of a student's demonstrated financial need. When calculating need, Dartmouth includes all of the costs of a Dartmouth education including tuition, room, board, books, fees, funds for some other living expenses, and travel for students who live far away from campus. Every student's financial need is reassessed each year, and the financial aid package is adjusted as necessary. Financial need is the difference between the calculated family contribution and the student's cost of attendance for the academic year.

Financial Documentation required

If applying for financial aid submit the CSS Profile, Non-Custodial Parent Profile, signed income and benefits statement from parents' employers and the student's tax return or Non-filling Statement if appropriate.

Freshman Profile Class of 2015

SAT Critical Reading 25th Percentile 670 75th Percentile 780
SAT Math 25th Percentile 680 75th Percentile 780
SAT Writing 25th Percentile 680 75th Percentile 790
ACT Median 33   ACT 25/75 percentile scores 30-34

Name:	Drexel University
Location:	Philadelphia, Pennsylvania
Website:	www.drexel.edu
US News & World 2012:	88 (tied)
QS Ranking 2012:	451-500
THE Ranking 2011-12:	226-250
Admission Profile:	No need-based aid, n/a
Cost of attendance:	$63,615 (2012-2013)
Tuition element of cost:	$41,500
Admission rate:	55%
Admission deadline:	January 15
Scholarship deadline:	January 15
Common App®:	Yes
Advanced credit:	Higher IB
	A Level possibly by review

International student financial support:
Drexel does not provide need-based financial aid to international students. International students are eligible for merit-based awards and scholarships.

Financial Documentation required
I-20 Application Form confirming source of funds. Drexel prefers this to be submitted with application but this is not an absolute requirement. It must be submitted before admission is finalised.

Dean's Scholarships
Drexel awards a limited number of Dean's Scholarships to international undergraduate students who have excellent academic credentials and the potential for high academic achievement. These scholarships are very competitive and are only offered upon admission to Drexel. Students must maintain a 3.0 GPA to retain their scholarship.
Award: partial tuition which is renewable. The number of awards varies.

Freshman Profile Class of 2015
Average SAT Math (25/75 percentiles) 560–670
Average SAT Critical Reading (25/75 percentiles) 530–630
Average SAT Writing scores (25/75 percentiles) 520–630

Name:	Duke University
Location:	Durham, North Carolina
Website:	www.duke.edu
US News & World 2012:	10
QS Ranking 2012:	20
THE Ranking 2011-12:	22
Admission Profile:	Need-aware if applying for financial aid.
	Need-blind if no application for financial aid.
Cost of attendance:	$59,343 (2012-2013)
Tuition element of cost:	$44,101
Admission rate:	13%
Admission deadline:	January 2
Scholarship deadline:	varies
Common App®:	Yes
Advanced credit:	Higher IB and A Level

International student financial support:
Duke University will meet full demonstrated financial need for a limited number of international students applying for first-year admission. Financial resources for these students are limited and each year Duke expects to enroll 20-25 first-year foreign citizens who receive need-based financial aid.

There are two applicant pools for foreign nationals: those not applying for financial aid who will be considered for admission along with US citizens and Lawful Permanent Residents, and those applying for financial aid who will be considered in a separate process for a limited number of places in the entering class. Also, foreign citizens who do not apply for financial aid initially may not subsequently apply for financial aid during their time at Duke unless they become U.S. citizens or permanent residents. Every applicant to Duke University is considered for various merit scholarships. Duke has a 4-year award policy for international students. If you attend Duke, your parent and student contributions will be exactly the same each year even though the cost of attendance will increase from year to year. This means that the aid from Duke will increase to cover any increase in the anticipated cost of education, but your parent and student contributions will not change.

Financial Documentation required
If applying for aid submit the CSS Profileand parents tax return for most recent year or certified statement of tax and earnings from employer.

Angier B. Duke Memorial Scholarship Program
See chapter five

Karsh International Scholarships

International undergraduate applicants to Duke who have demonstrated need will be considered for the Karsh Scholarship. Karsh Scholars may also apply for support for necessities, such as computers.

Award: tuition, room and board, mandatory fees, and demonstrated need that exceeds those costs. In addition the scholarship covers up to $7000 of funding for research/service opportunities during the three summers prior to graduation. Number of awards: varies, more than 4 in 2011-2012.

Reginaldo Howard Memorial Scholarship

The Reginaldo Howard Memorial Scholarship is awarded annually to students of African heritage who have demonstrated outstanding leadership ability, scholastic achievement, community involvement, and evidence of serious commitment to a life of service to others. There is no application process for this scholarship; potential candidates are identified by the Office of Admissions. All scholars must maintain a respectable GPA annually to continue the benefits of the scholarship. Additionally, "Reggie" Scholars are offered up to $5,000 for research or other educational enrichment programmes. The R. Howard scholarship award is tuition and mandatory fees including room and board. Number of awards: varies

Robertson Scholars Program

See chapter five

University Scholars Program

There is no separate application process and all eligible students are considered. Scholars are selected partly on the basis of financial need and Duke will meet 100% of the demonstrated need not covered by the award. Award: full tuition for four years, funding for summer abroad or intensive research experience after year 3, one or two semesters of study abroad. Number of awards: up to 8 per year

Alumni Endowed Scholars

Available to children or grandchildren of Duke alumni who are accepted for undergraduate admission to Duke University and who demonstrate financial need. Covering full-tuition the scholarship is awarded on the basis of academic achievement, leadership performance and meritorious activity outside the classroom.

Freshman Profile Class of 2015

Middle 50% for Accepted Students in Arts

SAT Critical Reading 680-780	SAT Math 690-790
SAT Writing 690-790	ACT Composite 31-34

Middle 50% for Accepted Students Sciences/Engineering

SAT Critical Reading 690-770	SAT Math 760-800
SAT Writing 710-790	ACT Composite 33-35

Name:	Emory University
Location:	Atlanta, Georgia
Website:	www.emory.edu
US News & World 2012:	20
QS Ranking 2012:	122
THE Ranking 2011-12:	75
Admission Profile:	No need-based aid, n/a
Cost of attendance:	$58,887 (2011-2012)
Tuition element of cost:	$40,600
Admission rate:	27%
Admission deadline:	January 15
	November 15 if applying for merit scholarship
Scholarship deadline:	November 15
Common App®:	Yes
Advanced credit:	Higher IB
	A Level on case by case basis

International student financial support:

Emory does not provide need-based financial aid to international students. International students do qualify for merit-based aid.

Financial Documentation required

Emory's International Financial Information Form submitted as part of application for admission.

Emory Scholars Program

See chapter seven

Goizueta Scholars Award

Applicants should have superior academic credentials, a demonstrated interest in business, as evidenced by engagement in entrepreneurial activities, participation in internships, membership in business clubs, and/or involvement in business-related conferences, competitions, and similar offerings. Leadership and community service are also important components in the selection process, and candidates who bring diverse perspectives and backgrounds are of special interest.

Scholars have guaranteed admission to Emory's Goizueta Business School once they have junior standing. In the freshman and sophomore years, these students have the opportunity to enroll in special business scholar seminars and to participate in an extensive array of leadership and professional activities. Scholars have priority access to business classes and a wide variety of internships, mentoring, and other career services.

Alben W. Barkley (Debate) Scholarship
Students need to demonstrate academic achievement and debate excellence. Application required. Number of awards: one

Dean's Music Scholarships
Emory's Department of Music offers Dean's Music Scholarships to incoming first-year students who show exceptional promise in their applied areas of music. To be considered for one of these scholarships, you must first meet all admission requirements for Emory College and intend to major in music. All audition students are considered for the scholarship. Award: half-tuition. Number of awards: several each year

Freshman Profile Class of 2015
Admitted Students middle 50%
SAT verbal: 650-740
SAT math: 670-770
SAT writing: 660-750
SAT total: 2020–2220
ACT: 30-33

Name:	Fordham University
Location:	Bronx, New York
Website:	www.fordham.edu
US News & World 2012:	53 (tied)
QS Ranking 2012:	601+
THE Ranking 2011-12:	not listed
Admission Profile:	No need-based aid, n/a
Cost of attendance:	$66,117 (2012-2013)
Tuition element of cost:	$41,000
Admission rate:	51%
Admission deadline:	January 15
Scholarship deadline:	January 15
Common App®:	Yes
Advanced credit:	Higher IB, A Level, case by case basis

International student financial support:
Fordham does not provide need-based financial aid to international students, but does offer merit scholarships.

Financial Documentation required
Fordham's Application for Certificate of Eligibility (AFCOE) submitted after admission.

Merit Scholarships
All complete international applications for undergraduate admission are considered for merit scholarships. There is no separate scholarship application process. Competition is strong.

Dean's Scholarship
The strongest admitted students will be considered for this scholarship. Typically, recipients have an A/A- average, minimum 1400 SAT with an even split between the critical reading and math sections, with typically above a 2100 including the SAT Writing section. These students also usually have strong extracurricular involvement. Award: minimum of $10,000 annually. Number of awards: varies

Presidential Scholarship
Presidential scholars typically have an A average and rank within the top 1-2% of their high school graduating class. Recipients usually score above 2200 on the SAT and have strong extracurricular involvement and demonstration of leadership. Award: full tuition and board. Number of awards: 20

Freshman Profile Class of 2015
SAT I Middle 50% for Accepted students 1830-2050.
ACT Composite Middle 50% for Accepted students 27-31

Name:	George Washington University
Location:	Washington, D.C.
Website:	www.gwu.edu
US News & World 2012:	50 (tied)
QS Ranking 2012:	339
THE Ranking 2011-12:	135
Admission Profile:	No need-based aid, n/a
Cost of attendance:	$62,245 (2012-2013)
Tuition element of cost:	$45,735
Admission rate:	33%
Admission deadline:	January 10
Scholarship deadline:	January 10
Common App®:	Yes
Advanced credit:	Higher IB

International student financial support:
GW does not provide need-based financial aid to international students. Merit scholarships are available but limited. International applicants are automatically considered for merit scholarships when applying to GW and there is no separate scholarship application. Scholarships and merit awards can only be used towards tuition expenses, but are renewable for up to ten consecutive semesters providing students maintain full-time enrolment and make satisfactory academic progress.

Financial Documentation required
GW's Financial Certificate for International Students and bank statement.

Presidential International Scholarship
Any non-US citizen who is admitted to GW as a first-year undergraduate for the fall semester and has strong academic credentials is automatically considered for this Scholarship. This scholarship award amount varies, up to full tuition.

Engineering Scholarships
The School of Engineering and Applied Sciences offers a generous programme of scholarships through the Presidential Academic Scholarship Program and all applicants are considered for these awards at the time of admission. The award of the scholarship is contingent upon enrolling in the School of Engineering and Applied Science. A larger pool of funds for engineering awards allows approximately 50% of engineering and computer science freshmen to receive a scholarship. Award amount varies as does the number of scholarships awarded.

Freshman Profile Class of 2015
Mid 50 percent SAT range: 1900-2100
Mid 50 percent ACT range: 28-31

Name:	Georgetown University
Location:	Washington, D.C.
Website:	www.georgetown.edu
US News & World 2012:	22
QS Ranking 2012:	183 (tied)
THE Ranking 2011-12:	138
Admission Profile:	Need-aware
Cost of attendance:	$60,080 (2012-2013)
Tuition element of cost:	$42,360
Admission rate:	17%
Admission deadline:	January 10
Scholarship deadline:	February 1
Common App®:	No
Advanced credit:	Higher IB and A Level

International student financial support:
Prospective international students who wish to be considered for need-based financial aid should indicate their interest on the application for undergraduate admission and must submit a CSS Profile online. Admitted students who have requested financial aid and are not U.S. citizens or permanent residents will be considered for a very limited number of need-based scholarships.

Financial Documentation required
If applying for need-based financial support students must submit the CSS Profile and the Non-Custodial Parent Statement.

Georgetown Undergraduate Scholarships
GU's Undergraduate Scholarship Program provides need-based awards to eligible undergraduates to meet 100% of their demonstrated financial need for scholarship (grant) assistance. A portion of the scholarship assistance is funded by benefactors and is given through named awards to students who meet the additional selection preferences specified by the donors. Students apply for GU Scholarships, including those named by donors, by completing the standard applications for need-based financial aid at Georgetown. Awards range in value from $1,000 to more than $50,000 per year, depending on the student's eligibility for scholarship assistance

Georgetown's Incentive Scholarships
These awards are designed to assist talented undergraduates, and are often made to students who are pursuing certain academic or extra-curricular interests.
Georgetown Incentive Scholarship awards typically reduce the expected family contribution and/or the student loan or work components of a standard need-based Georgetown financial aid package.
Students may apply by completing the applications for need-based financial aid at Georgetown and by following supplemental application/selection procedures.

1789 Scholarships
Named in honour of the year Georgetown was founded.
Award: $3,000 per year in loan relief (students receive less loan and more grant aid) and budget relief for need-based Georgetown scholarship aid in amounts up to $22,000 per year.
John Carroll Scholarships
Candidates for these scholarships are nominated by the GU Office of Undergraduate Admissions based on their exceptionally distinguished high school records and their demonstrated financial need. Students who applied for need-based GU financial aid are nominated by the GU Admissions office. Award: $3,000 renewable annually
The Pedro Arrupe, S.J. Scholarship for Peace
This scholarship was established by generous donors to enable international students with financial need, especially those from socially conflicted areas of the world, to receive a Jesuit education at Georgetown. Recipients are selected from the pool of international students who have been admitted to the University, on the recommendation of the University admissions committees. Awards vary.
The Sultan Qaboos bin-Said Arabic Language and Culture Scholarship
This scholarship fund was created by His Majesty Sultan Qaboos bin-Said of Oman to provide scholarships to selected Arabic majors. Further information about the programme is available from the Office of the Dean of the Georgetown University Faculty of Languages and Linguistics or the GU Arabic Department.
The President Anwar El Sadat Memorial Scholarship
The Anwar El Sadat Scholarship was established to bring Egyptian students requiring need-based aid to Georgetown University to earn an undergraduate degree (in the school of their choosing) provided they return to Egypt upon completion of their degree.
The Tatung Institute of Technology Scholarship
The Tatung Institute of Technology established this scholarship to pay the tuition of a student who requires aid and is a citizen of the Republic of China, who is obliged to return to Taiwan to serve at the Tatung Institute. This scholarship is restricted to students enrolled in the Languages and Linguistics division of the College.
Freshman Profile Class of 2015
SAT - Critical Reading 670-770   SAT - Math 660-770

Name:	Georgia Institute of Technology
Location:	Atlanta, Georgia
Website:	www.gatech.edu
US News & World 2012:	36
QS Ranking 2012:	88
THE Ranking 2011-12:	24
Admission Profile:	No need-based aid, n/a
Cost of attendance:	$40,568 (2012-2013)
Tuition element of cost:	$26,148
Admission rate:	51%
Admission deadline:	December 15
Scholarship deadline:	n/a
Common App®:	No
Advanced credit:	Higher IB

International student financial support:
Georgia Tech does not provide need-based or merit-based financial aid to international students.

Financial Documentation required
Documents verifying funds are submitted admission has been offered.

Freshman Profile Class of 2015
Mid-50% GPA: 3.76 - 4.07
Mid-50% SAT: 1940 - 2160
Mid-50% ACT: 28-32

Name:	Harvard University
Location:	Cambridge, Massachusetts
Website:	www.harvard.edu
US News & World 2012:	1 (tied)
QS Ranking 2012:	3
THE Ranking 2011-12:	2
Admission Profile:	Need-blind
Cost of attendance:	$65,118 (2012-2013)
Tuition element of cost:	$37,567
Admission rate:	6%
Admission deadline:	January 1
	December 1 onwards recommended for international students
Scholarship deadline:	n/a
Common App®:	Yes
Advanced credit:	Higher IB and A Level

International student financial support:
The financial aid policies for foreign citizens are exactly the same as those for U.S. citizens. All aid is need-based, and admissions decisions are made without regard to whether an applicant has applied for financial assistance. As an Ivy League university, there are no academic, athletic, or merit-based awards. Harvard will meet the demonstrated need of every student, for all four years. Changes to Harvard's financial aid policy has dramatically reduced the amount families with incomes below $150,000 (about £92,000) are expected to pay, and parents of families with incomes below $65,000 (about £40,000) are not expected to contribute at all to college costs. Home equity and retirement funds are not considered as a resource in the determination of a family contribution, and aid packages do not include any loans. Admitted students who apply for assistance will receive a financial aid award at the time of their admission in early April. The Financial Aid Committee carefully considers each admitted student's family financial circumstances and strives to ensure that a Harvard education remains fully accessible to those talented students that have been admitted. Each student's demonstrated financial need is fully met with a combination of jobs and scholarship assistance. There is a specific website for students applying from the UK - http://www.harvard-ukadmissions.co.uk/
Financial Documentation required
If applying for aid CSS Profile and Non-custodial Parent Profile
All international students must submit Harvard's Financial Statement for Students from Foreign Countries.

Freshman Profile Class of 2015

Test Score Ranges (Mid 50%)

Scores are represented as low score | average score | high score:

SAT I Verbal: 690 | 745 | 800

SAT I Math: 700 | 745 | 790

SAT Combined: 2,075 | 2,225 | 2,375

ACT English: 32 | 33 | 35

ACT Math: 31 | 33 | 35

ACT Composite: 31 | 32 | 34

Name:	**Indiana University**
Location:	**Bloomington, Indiana**
Website:	**www.iub.edu**
US News & World 2012:	**75 (tied)**
QS Ranking 2012:	**210**
THE Ranking 2011-12:	**123**
Admission Profile:	No need-based aid, n/a
Cost of attendance:	$47,008 (2012-2013)
Tuition element of cost:	$31,647
Admission rate:	72%
Admission deadline:	April 1
	November 1 for automatic academic scholarship consideration
Scholarship deadline:	November 1
Common App®:	No
Advanced credit:	Higher IB and A Level

International student financial support:
Indiana University does not provide need-based financial aid to international students. Admitted international freshmen students, who submit their completed admission application by November 1, will automatically be considered by the Office of Scholarships for Automatic Academic Scholarships. See below for specific information on students applying to the Jacob School of Music.

Financial Documentation required
IU's Declaration of Financial Support submitted as part of admission application.

Automatic Academic Scholarships
No separate application is required but to be considered for Automatic Academic Scholarships, students must submit all admission application materials by November 1. Awards are made on the basis of standardised test results and high school performance. The SAT score considered is based on the Critical Reading and Math sections only. The ACT score considered is the combined highest composite score. IU will only accept official test scores sent directly from the testing agencies. International students applying to the Jacob School of Music are also eligible for merit scholarships. In addition to the regular admission process and application deadline students also have to submit a performance recording or portfolio (for composition or recording arts) by the pre-screening submission deadline of December 1. Students may then be notified that they have to attend an on-campus audition/interview. Once admitted, students will be considered for Automatic Academic Scholarships administered by the Jacob School of Music. Scholarships are awarded on the basis of talent, academic achievement and department need.

The value and conditions of the scholarships are the same as those administered by the Office of Scholarships.

IU Distinction Scholarship

The IU Distinction Scholarship is awarded to the best and brightest out-of-state and international students who obtain a minimum SAT score of 1340 or minimum ACT of 30 and have a minimum high-school GPA of 3.80 on a 4.0 scale. These scholarship awards are $9000 annually, renewable for a total of four years provided recipient maintains a minimum IU cumulative 3.0 GPA and is enrolled-full-time. The number of awards varies.

IU Prestige Scholarship

The IU Prestige Scholarship is awarded to out-of-state and international students who obtain a minimum SAT score of 1220 or minimum ACT of 27 and have a minimum high-school GPA of 3.70 on a 4.0 scale. Award: $4000 annually, renewable for a total of four years provided recipient maintains a minimum IU cumulative 3.0 GPA and is enrolled-full-time. The number of awards varies.

Freshman Profile Class of 2015

SAT: middle 50%, Critical Reading and Math 1100-1290

ACT: middle 50%, composite 25-30

GPA: middle 50% 3.5–4.0

Name:	Iowa State University of Science & Technology
Location:	Ames, Iowa
Website:	www.iastate.edu
US News & World 2012:	97 (tied)
QS Ranking 2012:	319
THE Ranking 2011-12:	184
Admission Profile:	No need-based aid, n/a
Cost of attendance:	$33,280 (2012-2013)
Tuition element of cost:	$19,838
Admission rate:	90%
Admission deadline:	March 1
	January 1 for best scholarship consideration
Scholarship deadline:	January 1
Common App®:	No
Advanced credit:	Higher and Subsidary IB

International student financial support:
Iowa State does not provide need-based financial aid to international students. International students are expected to fund their own education but can apply for merit scholarships that do not have US citizenship requirements or do not require students to have applied for need-based aid.

Financial Documentation required
Financial Statement for international applicants submitted as part of admission application.

International Student Ambassador Scholarships
Awards are made to students with exceptional leadership qualities and a desire to positively represent both their home country and Iowa State to prospective students. After admission to Iowa State, students must submit a specific application by the April 1 deadline. An essay is required describing leadership experiences, community service, volunteering and why the applicant is interested in assisting Iowa State with international recruitment. Scholarships are renewable until graduation provided the recipient maintains a 2.0 GPA, full time enrolment and serves as an Ambassador for at least 2 semesters.

Award: three different levels. Gold $7,000 per year (renewable); Cardinal $5,000 per year (renewable); Leadership up to $4,000 per year (renewable). The number of awards varies.

Wessman Scholarships
All admitted freshmen who have declared either Agricultural Engineering (AE) or Agricultural Systems Technology (AST) as their major will be considered automatically. The selection of these awards is based primarily on ACT composite

%and math scores, high school rank and grade point average, leadership activities and honors. The award amount varies. Up to 12 scholarships are awarded.

Freshman Profile Class of 2015

ACT Composite Scores

75th percentile   27.8

Mean   24.9

25th percentile   22.0

Name:	The Johns Hopkins University
Location:	Baltimore, Maryland
Website:	www.jhu.edu
US News & World 2012:	13
QS Ranking 2012:	16
THE Ranking 2011-12:	14
Admission Profile:	Need-aware
Cost of attendance:	$66,150 (2012-2013)
Tuition element of cost:	$43,930
Admission rate:	18%
Admission deadline:	January 1
Scholarship deadline:	March 1
Common App®:	Yes
Advanced credit:	Higher IB and A Level

International student financial support:
JHU offers need-based and merit-based scholarships to undergraduate international students. As funds are limited JHU takes financial need into consideration when making the admissions decision. If an applicant applies for financial aid and is determined to have financial need, JHU will offer admission to that student only if funds are available to meet that student's financial need. International students who are not offered scholarship assistance for their first year will not be eligible for scholarship assistance for any other academic period while they are undergraduates at JHU.

Financial Documentation required
International Student Certification of Finances submitted as part of international applicantion. CSS Profile to be submitted by March 1 if unable to provide proof of sufficient funds and you are requesting need-based financial aid.

Johns Hopkins International Student Scholarships
JHU offers renewable scholarships to incoming international freshman. Eligibility is based on financial need and merit. Students must submit the CSS Profile to be considered. The amount varies depending on the financial need of the student. A 3.0 GPA must be maintained to renew the scholarship. Prospective students must complete the Johns Hopkins International Student Application to be considered.

The Hodson Trust Scholarships
Awarded on the basis of academic and personal achievement, leadership, and contribution. The scholarships are automatically renewed each year, provided the recipient maintains a 3.0 grade point average.
Award: up to $23,00 annually. Number of awards: maximum of 20

Charles R. Westgate Scholarship in Engineering
Merit-based scholarship provide for four years of undergraduate study in engineering. Freshman applicants indicating an engineering major may be considered for the scholarships if they can demonstrate an outstanding high school record and achievements in other areas including leadership, success in science fairs, and evidence of independent research.
Award: full tuition per year and a stipend toward living expenses
Number of awards: 2

Freshman Profile Class of 2015
Middle 50th percentile for admitted students
SAT CR: 670-750
SAT Math: 690-780
SAT Writing: 670-770
ACT: 30-34

Name:	**Lehigh University**
Location:	**Bethlehem, Pennsylvania**
Website:	**www.lehigh.edu**
US News & World 2012:	**38 (tied)**
QS Ranking 2012:	**501-550**
THE Ranking 2011-12:	**301-350**
Admission Profile:	Need-aware
Cost of attendance:	$55,670 (2012-2013)
Tuition element of cost:	$41,920
Admission rate:	33%
Admission deadline:	January 1
Scholarship deadline:	January 1
Common App®:	Yes
Advanced credit:	Higher IB and A Level

International student financial support:

Lehigh offers financial aid to international students on a very limited basis. Both merit-based and need-based aid is available and financial aid is competitive. In evaluating students for aid, Lehigh considers a combination of the student's academic & extracurricular achievements and the student/family need for financial assistance. The amount of financial aid a student receives is determined on an individual basis and it is not possible to estimate a financial aid package until Lehigh has received the complete admissions and financial aid applications. Need-based awards will be made in the form of a package, combining university grant aid, educational loan (repayable after the recipient is no longer enrolled on at least a half-time basis), and on-campus, part-time employment.

Financial Documentation required

International Student Certification of Finaces submitted with application
Submit CSS Profile or ISFAA (International Student Financial Aid Application) if applying for need-based aid.

Merit Scholarships

When awarding merit-based aid, Lehigh looks beyond academic talent alone. Recommendations, personal essays and student contributions outside the classroom are considered.

Academic Merit Awards

Lehigh's most prestigious merit award. No separate application is required and all admitted students are considered. Recipients must be in the top tier of the applicant pool. Criteria for selection includes high school (or equivalent) curriculum, SAT scores, and leadership activities. Renewable for four years provided that recipients maintain a GPA of 3.5 or higher.
Award amounts equate to either half or full tuition. The number of awards varies.

Dean's Scholars

Recipients are those who excel academically and demonstrate leadership. No separate application is required and all admitted students are considered. Renewable for four years provided that recipients maintain a GPA of 3.0 or higher. Award: $10,000 per year. The number of awards varies.

Lehigh Scholars

The Lehigh Scholars programme is a need-based merit award given to students with high academic merit and demonstrated need. All admitted students are considered. The number of awards varies.

Freshman Profile Class of 2015

Middle 50% of admitted students

SAT critical reading 610–710

SAT math   660–750

ACT (not including writing score)   29–32

Name:	Marquette University
Location:	Milwaukee, Wisconsin
Website:	www.marquette.edu
US News & World 2012:	82 (tied)
QS Ranking 2012:	601+
THE Ranking 2011-12:	not listed
Admission Profile:	No need-based aid, n/a
Cost of attendance:	$51,000 (2012-2013)
Tuition element of cost:	$32,810
Admission rate:	62%
Admission deadline:	April 1
Scholarship deadline:	February 1
Common App®:	Yes
Advanced credit:	Higher IB

International student financial support:
Marquette does not provide need-based financial aid to international students. International students are considered for financial scholarships at the time of admission and early application is recommended. Merit scholarships are used for payment of tuition.

Financial Documentation required
Financial Sponsorship Form submitted as part of application process.

Merit Scholarships
There is no separate application for most scholarships and the scholarship committee uses the information from the required application materials to make its decision. However, students may choose to send additional information to improve their prospects for admission and financial aid. Examples include verified information about academic rank or position in class, school or country, evidence of social involvement, leadership experience and service to others and a personal essay with information about background and plans for the future. All information submitted is considered in order to make the best possible admission and scholarship decisions.

International Jesuit High School Scholarship
Students who have attended an international Jesuit high school are eligible for scholarships covering half the tuition cost per academic year. These awards are renewable.

Kimberley-Clarke Scholars Award
Scholarships for international students from the 34 countries where Kimberley-Clarke has a presence who wish to major in biology, chemistry, computer science, math, business or engineering. For the Class of 2015 the award was $4000 per year.

101

The Pere Marquette Explorer Scholarship
Established in the spirit of exploration and discovery that was demonstrated by the university's namesake, this scholarship seeks to draw students from diverse geographic backgrounds. This annual scholarship of $5,000 is offered to 12 freshmen.

Ignatius Scholarships for International Students
See chapter six.

Freshman Profile Class of 2015
ACT Middle 50%: 24–29
SAT Middle 50%: 1070–1260

Name:	Massachusetts Institute of Technology
Location:	Boston, Massachusetts
Website:	www.mit.edu
US News & World 2012:	5 (tied)
QS Ranking 2012:	1
THE Ranking 2011-12:	7
Admission Profile:	Need-blind
Cost of attendance:	$57,010 (2012-2013)
Tuition element of cost:	$41,770
Admission rate:	10%
Admission deadline:	January 1 (December 10 for scheduling optional interview)
Scholarship deadline:	n/a
Common App®:	No
Advanced credit:	Higher IB and A Level

International student financial support:
Every year more than 3,000 international students apply to MIT, and fewer than 150 are admitted. MIT intentionally limits the number of international students accepted because of their generous financial aid policy. MIT is one of the few schools in the world that offers need-blind admissions and meets the full demonstrated financial need for all admitted students, including international ones. MIT does not offer merit scholarships; all financial support is need-based.

Financial Documentation required
If applying for need-based aid submit the CSS online profile by February 15.

Freshman Profile Class of 2015
Middle 50% score range of admitted students:
SAT Math 740, 800
SAT Critical Reading 680, 780
SAT Writing 690, 780
SAT Subject Test - Math 750, 800
SAT Subject Test - Science 720,800
ACT Math 34, 36
ACT English 32, 35
ACT Composite 32, 35

Name:	Miami University
Location:	Oxford, Ohio
Website:	www.muohio.edu
US News & World 2012:	90 (tied)
QS Ranking 2012:	not listed
THE Ranking 2011-12:	not listed
Admission Profile:	Need-aware
Cost of attendance:	$42,339 (2011-2012)
Tuition element of cost:	$27,797
Admission rate:	78%
Admission deadline:	February 1
Scholarship deadline:	March 1
Common App®:	Yes
Advanced credit:	Higher level IB

International student financial support:
Miami does not provide need-based financial aid to international students. There are a limited number of merit scholarships and all international undergraduate applicants who complete their applications for admission by March 1 (for the fall semester. Many academic departments award scholarships to incoming freshmen. To be considered for a scholarship from the department in an intended major, applicants should contact the department chair and declare their intended major with the Office of Admission by early February.

Financial Documentation required
MU's International Student Financial Support Form with documentation providing proof of financial support submitted as part of application for admission.

International Education Scholarships
To be considered, students should have achieved outstanding academic records and competitive test scores. Although no separate application is required in order to be considered for an International Education Scholarship, all international applicants must still complete Sections A and B of the Confidential Financial Statement in the Common Application Supplement for International Students and submit supporting financial documentation. Award: up to $10,000 per year and renewable. The number of awards varies.

Harrison Scholarship
The Harrison Scholarship is Miami's premier scholarship programme.
To apply for the Harrison Scholarship, students must submit the Honours Application and the regular admission application to the Office of Admission by November 3. Prior Harrison Scholars averaged a 34 ACT and/or 1510 on the SAT CR+M, had a class rank in the top 2% and obtained near perfect grade point averages. In addition, many received some type of national award or recognition,

completed internships or research while in high school, and demonstrated excellent records of service and leadership. This scholarship is renewable with a 3.5 cumulative GPA. The scholarship is in-state tuition, fees and is renewable. The number of awards varies.

University Merit Scholarships
Miami University offers scholarship awards to new autumn first-year, full-time in-state (Ohio) and out-of-state students to recognize student achievement and to continue to make a high quality education more affordable for students. These awards are renewable for up to four years. The number of awards varies.

Freshman Profile Class of 2015
The average test score was a 30 ACT and 1340 on the SAT CR+M
Test scores ranged from 21 to 36 on the ACT and 990 to 1600 on the SAT CR+M.

Name:	Michigan State University
Location:	East Lansing, Michigan
Website:	www.msu.edu
US News & World 2012:	71 (tied)
QS Ranking 2012:	174
THE Ranking 2011-12:	96
Admission Profile:	No need-based aid, n/a
Cost of attendance:	$44,827 (2011-2012)
Tuition element of cost:	$31,757
Admission rate:	57%
Admission deadline:	rolling admission but international applicants recommended to apply by November 1
Scholarship deadline:	rolling admission but international applicants recommended to apply by November 1 for maximum scholarship consideration
Common App®:	No
Advanced credit:	Higher IB and A Level

International student financial support:

MSU does not provide need-based financial aid to international students. There are limited merit scholarships for international students.

Financial Documentation required

MSU's Affadavit of Support for Undergraduate International Students submitted after admission.

Scholarships for International Students

The following scholarships are awarded, pending available funding, to incoming international freshmen. No additional applications are required.

Global Neighbours Scholarship

Awarded to a limited number of international students displaying academic achievement. Recipients must maintain minimum 2.5 cumulative GPA. The academic records of all scholars will be reviewed at the end of the first two semesters of enrollment and thereafter each semester.

Award amounts to $4,000 per year, renewable and limited to eight consecutive semesters of enrollment as an undergraduate student.

Legacy Scholarship

Awarded to academically talented students with non-Michigan residency status for tuition purposes who are the dependents of MSU alumni. The award amounts vary.

Patricia A. Szymczyk Butler Expendable Scholarship Fund

Awarded to an international student who is a graduate of a high school in Poland. The award amounts vary.

Global Spartan Scholarship
Awarded to a limited number of international students displaying academic achievement. Award: $1,000 in first year of enrolment
Freshman Profile Class of 2016
Middle 50 percent of enrolled freshmen Composite ACT: 24-28
Middle 50 percent of enrolled freshmen SAT (CR+M): 1060-1270

Name:	New York University
Location:	New York, New York
Website:	www.nyu.edu
US News & World 2012:	33 (tied)
QS Ranking 2012:	43
THE Ranking 2011-12:	44
Admission Profile:	No need-based aid, n/a
Cost of attendance:	$61,907 (2012-2013)
Tuition element of cost:	$43,204
Admission rate:	38%
Admission deadline:	January 1
Scholarship deadline:	n/a
Common App®:	Yes
Advanced credit:	Higher IB and A Level

International student financial support:

NYU does not provide need-based or merit-based financial aid to international students. International students admitted to NYU will be expected to pay the entire cost of their education with their own resources.

It is not necessary to submit financial documents with an application for admission. The NYU Application for Certificate of Eligibility (AFCOE) must be completed online by students who are offered admission when they pay their enrolment deposit.

Financial Documentation required

NYU Application for Certificate of Eligibility sumitted when accepting offer of admission.

Freshman Profile Class of 2013

25th Percentile 75th Percentile

SAT I Critical Reading 610 710

SAT Math 600 720

SAT Writing 620 710

SAT Essay 8 10

ACT Composite 27 31

Name:	Northeastern University
Location:	Boston, Massachusetts
Website:	www.northeastern.edu
US News & World 2012:	62 (tied)
QS Ranking 2012:	451-500
THE Ranking 2011-12:	201-225
Admission Profile:	No need-based aid, n/a
Cost of attendance:	$58,533 (2012-2013)
Tuition element of cost:	$39,320
Admission rate:	38%
Admission deadline:	January 15
Scholarship deadline:	January 15
Common App®:	Yes
Advanced credit:	Higher IB
	A and AS Level

International student financial support:
Northeastern University does not provide need-based financial aid to international students. NU does however, have several competitive scholarship programmes that are open to international students.

Financial Documentation required
NU's Declaration and Certification of Finances (DCF) Form submitted with admission application.

Merit Scholarships
The top 25 percent of admitted freshman may be considered for competitive merit scholarships that reward outstanding academic achievement. There is no separate application process but students must submit their undergraduate admission application to NU by the regular decision deadline. Award amounts vary between $5,000 to $20,000 per year.

The International Scholars Award
The International Scholars Award is awarded by NU's Admissions Office to incoming freshman international students to reward their outstanding achievements. The scholarship is awarded for a maximum of eight semesters as long as the student maintains a 3.0 GPA. Award: from $5,000 to $15,000

The Northeastern University Scholars Program
Recipients have distinguished themselves academically, demonstrated curiosity and creativity that extend beyond the classroom to impact the world around them, and displayed an entrepreneurial approach. Award: full tuition. Number of awards vary, up to 50 per year.

Freshman Profile Class of 2015
Middle 50%
Combined SAT 1890-2140
SAT Critical Reading 620-700
SAT Math 660-730
SAT Writing 630-710

Name:	Northwestern University
Location:	Evanston, Illinois
Website:	www.northwestern.edu
US News & World 2012:	12
QS Ranking 2012:	27
THE Ranking 2011-12:	26
Admission Profile:	Need-aware
Cost of attendance:	$61,240 (2012-2013)
Tuition element of cost:	$43,380
Admission rate:	20%
Admission deadline:	January 2
Scholarship deadline:	February 15
Common App®:	Yes
Advanced credit:	Higher IB. A Levels reviewed on an individual basis

International student financial support:

Northwestern University offers need-based financial aid awards to a small group of international students. The amount of financial aid needed by an international applicant may also be a factor in a final admission decision. As a result of this need-aware approach and the limited funds available to students, Northwestern's acceptance rate for international applicants requesting aid is less favorable than the rate of acceptance for those students not requesting aid. Only those students who apply for and receive financial aid for their freshman year will be eligible to receive financial assistance in subsequent years. International students and their families will be expected to contribute towards educational expenses. Awards may be comprised of scholarship and/or loan. All scholarships and grants are need-based.

Financial Documentation required

Submit the CSS Profile, parents tax return for the most recent tax year and non-custodial parent profile.

Freshman Profile Class of 2013

25th Percentile and 75th Percentile

SAT Critical Reading 670 750

SAT Math 690 780

SAT Writing 670 760

ACT Composite 31 33

Name:	**The Ohio State University**
Location:	**Columbus, Ohio**
Website:	**www.osu.edu**
US News & World 2012:	**55 (tied)**
QS Ranking 2012:	**105**
THE Ranking 2011-12:	**57**
Admission Profile:	No need-based aid, n/a
Cost of attendance:	$42,408 (2011-2012)
Tuition element of cost:	$24,759
Admission rate:	63%
Admission deadline:	February 1
Scholarship deadline:	February 1
Common App®:	No
Advanced credit:	Higher IB

International student financial support:
OSU does not provide need-based financial aid to international students. There is one partial merit scholarship available to international students.

Financial Documentation required
OSU's Affidavit of financial support for international students submitted with application.

International Undergraduate Scholarship
The International Undergraduate Scholarship is offered on a competitive basis to qualified full-time, Columbus campus international freshmen (students who have not attended university since graduating from high school/secondary school). Qualified applicants are those with an ACT composite scores of 28 or higher or combined SAT Critical Reading and Math scores of 1260 or higher, and are applying for Fall semester entry.

Award: $5,000 ($20,000 four–year value), renewable for eight semesters provided that recipient maintains 2.5 or higher GPA, maintains satisfactory academic progress and continues to pay the non-resident tuition surcharge.
The number of awards varies.

Freshman Profile Class of 2015
SAT Critical Reading and Math score range (middle 50%): 1170–1320
ACT score range (middle 50%): 26–30

Name:	**Pennsylvania State University**
Location:	**University Park, Pennsylvania**
Website:	**www.psu.edu**
US News & World 2012:	**45 (tied)**
QS Ranking 2012:	**101**
THE Ranking 2011-12:	**51**
Admission Profile:	No need-based aid, n/a
Cost of attendance:	$49,300 (2012-2013)
Tuition element of cost:	$28,000
Admission rate:	26%
Admission deadline:	February 1
Scholarship deadline:	February 1
Common App®:	No
Advanced credit:	Higher level IB and A Level

International student financial support:
Penn State does not offer financial aid to international students.
Financial Documentation required
Financial Guarantee submitted after admission.
Freshman Profile Class of 2016
Middle 50% Combined SAT
University Park: 1750-1990; All other campuses: 1470-1720
Combined ACT
University Park: 26-30; All other campuses: 21-25
Combined English/Writing ACT
University Park: 25-30; All other campuses: 20-25

Name:	Pepperdine University
Location:	Malibu, California
Website:	www.pepperdine.edu
US News & World 2012:	55 (tied)
QS Ranking 2012:	not listed
THE Ranking 2011-12:	not listed
Admission Profile:	No need-based aid, n/a
Cost of attendance:	$60,222 (2012-2013)
Tuition element of cost:	$42,500
Admission rate:	38%
Admission deadline:	January 5
Scholarship deadline:	January 5
Common App®:	Yes
Advanced credit:	Higher IB

International student financial support:
Pepperdine University offers various scholarships for international students. There is no need-based financial aid available to international students.

Financial Documentation required
PU's International Student Data (ISD) form confirming financial support submitted with application.

The Presidential Scholars' Awards
All admitted students are automatically considered for the Presidential Scholars' Awards. A separate application is not necessary. The top 10-12% of all admitted applicants are awarded the scholarship each year. These scholarships are awarded to Fall semester applicants only. Awards vary.

The Lydia Hayne Scholarship Fund
This scholarship is offered only once every four years. Qualified applicants are a citizen of a country in Africa with an excellent academic record. Awards: tuition, room and board. Awards: one

Charles Lam Scholarship
This scholarship is for citizens of mainland China who wish to attend Seaver College of Arts. Available for entry in Fall and Spring semesters. Award is between $8,000 to $10,000 annually and is renewable. Number of awards: two or three per year

Freshman Profile Class of 2016
SAT Critical Reading, Math, and Writing 1808-2050 ACT Composite 27-31

Name:	Princeton University
Location:	Princeton, New Jersey
Website:	www.princeton.edu
US News & World 2012:	1 (tied)
QS Ranking 2012:	9
THE Ranking 2011-12:	5
Admission Profile:	Need-blind
Cost of attendance:	$59,130 (2012-2013)
Tuition element of cost:	$38,650
Admission rate:	9%
Admission deadline:	January 1
	December 15 recommended
Scholarship deadline:	n/a
Common App®:	Yes
Advanced credit:	Higher IB and A Level

International student financial support:
Princeton's financial aid policies for foreign citizens are exactly the same as those for U.S. citizens: need-blind admissions and need-based aid. "Need-blind" means that Princeton admits students on the basis of academic and personal promise, without regard to their ability to pay. "Need-based" means that financial aid packages are based on individual needs assessments. All financial aid is awarded on the basis of demonstrated financial need. As an Ivy League university, there are no academic, athletic, nor merit-based awards. Princeton believes that parents and students should pay what they reasonably can towards college expenses. The amount of this contribution varies and is based on their individual resources. Parental contributions are determined after a thorough review. Princeton uses its own need formula which takes into account numerous criteria. Each individual aid application is given careful consideration. Princeton will meet 100 percent of the demonstrated financial need with a combination of grants and on-campus employment.

Financial Documentation required
Princeton's Financial Aid Application and non-custodial parent profile to be submitted by February 1. Parents tax returns must be submitted by March 15.

Freshman Profile Class of 2015
Middle 50% scores

SAT Critical Reading 700-790	SAT Math 710-800
SAT Writing 700-790	ACT Composite 31-34

Name:	Purdue University
Location:	West Lafayette, Indiana
Website:	www.purdue.edu
US News & World 2012:	62 (tied)
QS Ranking 2012:	95
THE Ranking 2011-12:	98
Admission Profile:	No need-based aid, n/a
Cost of attendance:	$45,242 (2012-2013)
Tuition element of cost:	$32,412
Admission rate:	65%
Admission deadline:	January 15, but international students encouraged to apply earlier; some programmes have earlier deadlines
Scholarship deadline:	n/a
Common App®:	No
Advanced credit:	Higher IB and A Level

International student financial support:
Purdue does not offer need or merit-based financial aid to international students.

Financial Documentation required
Source of financial support is required when completing application form. Supporting documents submitted after admission.

Freshman Profile Class of 2015
Middle 50% SAT range: 1530-1910
Middle 50% ACT composite range: 24-40
Middle 50% ACT English/Writing range: 22-28

Name:	Rensselaer Polytechnic Institute
Location:	Troy, New York
Website:	www.rpi.edu
US News & World 2012:	50 (tied)
QS Ranking 2012:	296
THE Ranking 2011-12:	144
Admission Profile:	No need-based aid, n/a
Cost of attendance:	$61,020 (2012-2013)
Tuition element of cost:	$43,350
Admission rate:	40%
Admission deadline:	February 15
Scholarship deadline:	n/a
Common App®:	Yes
Advanced credit:	Higher IB

International student financial support:
Renselaer does not provide need-based financial aid to international students. International students may apply for the merit-based award, The Rensselaer Medal.

Financial Documentation required
RPI's International Student Financial Statement submitted as part of application for admission.

The Renssellaer Medal
Rensselaer Polytechnic Institute, in conjunction with high schools around the world, has awarded the Rensselaer Medal to promising secondary school students who have distinguished themselves in mathematics and science. Each participating high school is allowed to select one member of the junior class (equivalent to Lower Sixth) to be honored with the Rensselaer Medal Award. There are currently no schools in the UK listed as participating school but they can apply to be part of the programme.

Class of 2014 Medal Winner Profile

High school average: A

Average SAT Critical Reading and Math combined: 1423

Average SAT Math: 733

Average SAT Critical Reading: 690

Award: minimum of $15,000 per year for tuition, guaranteed for four years (five for Architecture). The number of awards varies. 16% of students who enrolled in Fall 2011 were medal winners

Freshman Profile Class of 2015
Middle 50% for composite SAT (M and CR) 1290-1470

Name:	Rice University
Location:	Houston, Texas
Website:	www.rice.edu
US News & World 2012:	17 (tied)
QS Ranking 2012:	120
THE Ranking 2011-12:	72
Admission Profile:	Need-aware
Cost of attendance:	$52,742 (2012-2013)
Tuition element of cost:	$34,900
Admission rate:	17%
Admission deadline:	January 1
Scholarship deadline:	January 1
Common App®:	Yes
Advanced credit:	Higher IB
	A Level reviewed on a case-by-case basis

International student financial support:
Rice University requires all international applicants to provide financial information in conjunction with the application for admission. Financial documents provide information that will place international applicants into one of two categories prior to the admission decision. Students who do not require aid are placed into the same pool with all other incoming freshman. As international aid funds are limited, students requiring aid will be in a more competitive category.

Financial Documentation required
Rice International Student Financial Statement submitted as part of application for admission by all international students. CSS Profile must be submitted if applying for financial aid. All admitted freshman applicants are automatically considered for merit-based scholarships, so that no separate application forms or interviews are necessary. The Office of Admissions notifies scholarship winners at the time of admission to the university. Merit based scholarships exclusive to outstanding international students:

Edgar Odell Lovett Scholarship
Outstanding international applicants.
Award: half tuition, renewable for four years

Allen International Scholarship
Outstanding applicants who are foreign nationals.
Award: full tuition - renewable for four years
Merit based scholarships available to all admitted students include:

Trustee Distinguished Scholarship
Students whose personal talents distinguish them within the pool of admitted applicants. Award ranges from $17,500 to $22,500 and is renewable for four years.
Trustee Diversity Scholarship
Students whose diverse life experiences and contributions to diverse groups distinguish them within the pool of admitted applicants.
Award ranges from $17,500 to $22,500 and is renewable for four years.
Century Scholars Program
Students who demonstrate an aptitude for research with a faculty mentor.
Award: $4,000 and is renewable for two years, plus a guaranteed research mentorship.
Barbara Jordan Scholarship
Students who have distinguished themselves through initiatives that build bridges between cultural, racial, and ethnic groups.
Award ranges from $17,500 to $22,500 and is renewable for four years.
Engineering Scholarship
Outstanding applicants to the engineering division.
Award ranges from $7,500 to full tuition and is renewable for four years.
Freshman Profile Class of 2016
Middle 50% of SAT and ACT Scores for Accepted Students
SAT (Critical Reading + Math) 1430-1540
ACT 32-35

119

Name:	Rutgers, The State University of New Jersey
Location:	New Brunswick, New Jersey
Website:	www.rutgers.edu
US News & World 2012:	68 (tied)
QS Ranking 2012:	260
THE Ranking 2011-12:	81
Admission Profile:	No need-based aid, n/a
Cost of attendance:	$38,098 (2012-2013)
Tuition element of cost:	$22,766
Admission rate:	57%
Admission deadline:	December 1 November 1 for merit scholarships
Scholarship deadline:	December 1
Common App®:	No
Advanced credit:	Higher IB

International student financial support:

Rutgers does not provide need-based financial aid to international students. Some of the most academically accomplished international applicants may be offered merit scholarships.

Financial Documentation required

Rutger's International Student Financial Statement (ISFS) must be submitted at the time of application with supporting documents.

International Student Scholarships

No separate application is required and selections is very competitive. Awards are made for a total of four years and are renewed each year subject to a minimum 3.0 GPA. Award: varies. Number of awards: varies

Freshman Profile Class of 2015

Middle 50% of Regularly-Admitted Students New Brunswick Campus
SAT I Scores Critical Reading + Math + Writing
Arts and Sciences 1710-2000, School of the Arts 1690-1920
School of Environmental and Biological Sciences 1690-1980
School of Engineering 1820-2120, School of Pharmacy 2075-2250
Rutgers Business School 1860-2090
ACT Scores
School of Arts and Sciences 25-30, School of the Arts 25-29
School of Environmental and Biological Sciences 25-30
School of Engineering 27-32 School of Pharmacy 31-34
Rutgers Business School: Undergraduate - New Brunswick 28-32

Name:	Saint Louis University
Location:	St. Louis, Missouri
Website:	www.slu.edu
US News & World 2012:	90 (tied)
QS Ranking 2012:	not listed
THE Ranking 2011-12:	not listed
Admission Profile:	Need-aware
Cost of attendance:	$53,438 (2012-2013)
Tuition element of cost:	$34,740
Admission rate:	72%
Admission deadline:	February 1
Scholarship deadline:	December 1
Common App®:	Yes
Advanced credit:	Higher IB
	A Level by review

International student financial support:
SLU offers limited need-based financial support to incoming international freshman students. There are merit scholarships available to international students.
Financial Documentation required
SLU's International Student Financial Aid Application and supporting documents must be submitted with the application for admission. Scholarships with automatic consideration:
Billiken, Ignatian, University, Deans' and Vice Presidents' Scholarships
These four-year merit-based scholarships do not require a separate scholarship application. The application forFreshman Admission automatically qualifies applicants for consideration. After the priority deadline, scholarships will be awarded as funds are available. Awards range from $3,000 to $16,000 per year. The number of awards varies.
Jesuit High School Award
All applicants who graduate from a Jesuit high school and submit their completed application for admission by December 1 will automatically receive SLU's Jesuit High School Award. Award: $3,000 per year, which can be combined with other merit scholarships up to a maximum of the cost of full tuition.
Presidential Scholarship
Recipients of the Presidential Scholarship represent some of the most exemplary student leaders on SLU's campus. Students who meet the following minimum requirements are invited to complete the online application: minimum high school 3.85 GPA; minimum score of 30 on the ACT or 1330 (math and critical reading) on the SAT. Standardized test scores from the December test are the last exams that can be used to determine eligibility. Students meeting the initial eligibility

requirements must submit all components of Freshman Admission Application, including official high school transcript, test scores and Secondary School Report Form, by the priority deadline. Students must also submit a completed Presidential Scholarship Application, including scholarship essay, resume and two letters of recommendation. Upon review of the applicants, a select group of students will be invited to Saint Louis University's campus in January or February to interview and compete for the Presidential Scholarship. Award: full tuition, renewable. The number of awards varies.

Martin Luther King Jr. Scholarship

The Martin Luther King Jr. Scholarship is granted to students who are committed to the promotion of diversity in society and who demonstrate leadership in the classroom, on campus and in the greater community. Students are invited to complete the online application for the Martin Luther King Jr. Scholarship. Successful applicants possess a ranking in the upper third of the student's high school class; above average ACT or SAT test scores; cumulative high school GPA of 3.25 or higher, weighted or unweighted. Standardized test scores from the December test are the last that can be used to determine eligibility. Students meeting the initial eligibility requirements must submit all components of the Application for Freshman Admission, including official high school transcript, test scores and Secondary School Report Form, by January 15 and submit a completed Martin Luther King Jr. Scholarship Application, including scholarship essay, resume and two letters of recommendation, by January 15. Award: $3,000 per year that combines with other merit-based scholarships awarded by SLU. All MLK Scholars will receive a minimum total award of $13,000 per year (merit-based scholarship + MLK scholarship). The number of awards varies.

Freshman Profile Class of 2015

Test Score Ranges (Mid 50%)

Scores presented: low score | average score | high score

SAT I Verbal: 540 | 600 | 660   SAT I Math: 550 | 615 | 680

SAT Combined: 1,625 | 1,812 | 2,000

ACT English: 24 | 28 | 32   ACT Math: 24 | 27 | 30

ACT Composite: 24 | 27 | 30

Name:	**Southern Methodist University**
Location:	**Dallas, Texas**
Website:	**www.smu.edu**
US News & World 2012:	**62 (tied)**
QS Ranking 2012:	**601+**
THE Ranking 2011-12:	**not listed**
Admission Profile:	No need-based aid, n/a
Cost of attendance:	$58,085 (2012-2013)
Tuition element of cost:	$41,750
Admission rate:	54%
Admission deadline:	January 15
Scholarship deadline:	January 15
Common App®:	Yes
Advanced credit:	Higher IB and A Level

International student financial support:
SMU does not provide need-based financial aid to international students. All applicants are considered for merit scholarships. There is no separate application process for merit scholarships.

Financial Documentation required
Proof of finances submitted after admission.

President's Scholarship
These scholarships are the highest academic merit awards given by SMU. To be eligible students must have achieved an SAT score of at least 1350 (700 critical reading, 650 math) or a composite ACT score of 31 or higher. Candidates usually exhibit a high degree of intellectual curiosity, will have pursued the most rigorous high school coursework available and possess a record of exceptional school and/or community involvement. All admitted students are automatically reviewed and selected candidates are invited to interview. Award: full tuition and fees, renewable subject to maintaining a minimum 3.3 GPA. Number of awards is between 20 to 30 per year.

International Baccalaureate Scholars Program
A unique, culturally enriching programme for qualifying graduates of the IB Diploma Programme. Some IB Scholars will be eligible for financial rewards based on scholars' IB diploma exam scores. Programme membership is renewable through four years with a minimum 3.0 SMU GPA at the end of each spring semester. Awards: from $4,000 to $12,000 annually, or up to the cost of tuition and fees. The number of awards varies.

SMU Distinguished Scholars Program
Recipients must possess a strong academic background and a well-rounded extracurricular profile. The scholarship is renewable with a minimum 3.00 GPA. Award is up to $7,500 per year for 4 years. Number of awards vary.

Departmental Scholarships
In addition to merit scholarships, SMU offers departmental scholarships which are awarded based on the student's first major. Award amounts vary. The number of awards varies.

BBA Scholars Program
Admitted students who indicated Business as their primary academic interest will be automatically reviewed. Selection is based on academic merit. BBA Scholars are also automatically considered for renewable Business Scholarships, which are awarded to approximately 50 students.

Dedman College Scholars Program
Selected students are invited to apply to the Dedman College Scholars Program. Candidates will have a primary major within the Dedman College of Humanities and Sciences, strong SAT or ACT scores, have pursued a challenging high school curriculum as well as extracurricular involvement. The application process consists of a written application and an interview by a committee of Dedman College faculty, staff, and Dedman College Scholars. Renewable for four years provided the student maintains a 3.3 GPA, full-time enrolment in a Dedman College major, and engages in an approved research project.

Freshman Profile Class of 2015
SAT/ACT are not required for foreign passport holders, but will be considered if they are submitted as part of the application for admission. Scores are represented as low score | average score | high score

SAT I Verbal: 560 | 615 | 670
SAT I Math: 580 | 630 | 680
SAT Combined: 1,700 | 1,857 | 2,015
ACT English: 25 | 28 | 32
ACT Math: 25 | 28 | 31
ACT Composite: 25 | 27 | 30

Name:	Stanford University
Location:	Palo Alto, California
Website:	www.stanford.edu
US News & World 2012:	5 (tied)
QS Ranking 2012:	15
THE Ranking 2011-12:	2
Admission Profile:	Need-aware
Cost of attendance:	$58,846 (2012-2013)
Tuition element of cost:	$41,250
Admission rate:	7%
Admission deadline:	January 1
Scholarship deadline:	n/a
Common App®:	Yes
Advanced credit:	Higher level IB and A Level

International student financial support:
Financial aid at Stanford is based on demonstrated need, and Stanford makes every effort to meet the full computed need of all admitted students. However, because of the limited financial aid resources available to international students, Stanford can offer admission with financial aid to only a small number of international applicants a year. Thus, a student's request for financial aid may be a factor in the admission decision. Stanford will not admit a student unless it is certain that the student is self-funded or that Standford is able to provide financial aid. International students who do not request consideration for financial aid at the time they apply for admission will not be eligible to apply for aid at Stanford throughout their undergraduate years.
There are no merit scholarships - all financial support is need-based.
Financial Documentation required
Stanford's International Student Certification of Finances by February 15
CSS Profile if applying for need-based aid submitted by February 15.
Freshman Profile Class of 2015
25th/75th percentile

SAT Critical Reading 670 770	SAT Math 690 780
SAT Writing 680 780	
ACT Composite 30 34	ACT Math 30 35
ACT English 31 35	ACT Writing 29 32

Name:	**Stevens Institute of Technology**
Location:	**Hoboken, New Jersey**
Website:	**www.stevens.edu**
US News & World 2012:	**88 (tied)**
QS Ranking 2012:	**601+**
THE Ranking 2011-12:	**not listed**
Admission Profile:	No need-based aid, n/a
Cost of attendance:	$54,585 (2012-2013)
Tuition element of cost:	$41,942
Admission rate:	38%
Admission deadline:	January 15
Scholarship deadline:	January 15
Common App®:	No
Advanced credit:	Higher IB and A Level

International student financial support:
Stevens does not provide need-based financial aid to international students. All applicants are considered for merit scholarships. There is no separate application process for merit scholarships.

Financial Documentation required
Proof of finances submitted after admission.

The Edwin A. Stevens Scholarship
The Edwin A. Stevens Scholarship is named in honour of the Institute's founder. Students may be eligible for this award if they have a demonstrated record of excellence in high school as evidenced by grade point average, class rank, SAT scores and recommendations. Awards vary.

The Women in Engineering and Science Scholarship
Martha Bayard Stevens Scholarship
These scholarships are available to outstanding, scholarly female students with leadership qualities in all fields of study at Stevens. Awards vary.

The Ann P. Neupauer Scholarship
The Ann P. Neupauer Scholarship honours a selected academically-talented student with a four-year, full-tuition award.

Debaun Performing Arts Scholarship.
Students demonstrating achievement in performance, including drama or music, are considered for selection. Recipients of this scholarship will be awarded between $1,000-$5,000 per year, based on outstanding academic achievement, an essay, and either a performance resume, video, CD, or letter of recommendation that highlights your accomplishments

Other available awards include the
Becton Dickinson/Wesley J. Howe Scholarship
President's Award
Scholar of Excellence Award
Society of Automotive Engineers Scholarship
Science and Technology Center Volunteer Scholarship.
Class Profile:
Test Scores -- 25th / 75th Percentile
SAT Critical Reading: 560 / 660
SAT Math: 630 / 720
SAT Writing: 560 / 660
SAT Range: 1210-1400
Average GPA: 3.8

Name:	**SUNY College of Environmental Science and Forestry**
Location:	**Syracuse, New York**
Website:	**www.esf.edu**
US News & World 2012:	**82 (tied)**
QS Ranking 2012:	**601+**
THE Ranking 2011-12:	**not listed**
Admission Profile:	No need-based aid, n/a
Cost of attendance:	$33,368 (2012-2013)
Tuition element of cost:	$14,320
Admission rate:	47%
Admission deadline:	February 1
Scholarship deadline:	February 1
Common App®:	Yes
Advanced credit:	Higher IB

International student financial support:

ESF does not provide need-based financial aid to international students. International students will be considered for academic merit-based scholarships, assistantships and fellowships. A separate scholarship application is not required. International students are not eligible for admission to programs at The Ranger School.

Financial Documentation required

Proof of finances submitted after admission.

Presidential Scholarship Program

Outstanding high school seniors, including international students are eligible for the Presidential Scholarship. Students must submit an application no later than February 1. Past winners have achieved a combined SAT Math and Reading score of over 1200 or 27 on the ACT and excellent grades in high school. Awards are up to $8000 for out-of-state students. ESF awards over 100 student awards each year.

Freshman Profile of 2015

Test Scores -- 25th / 75th Percentile

SAT Critical Reading: 530 / 630

SAT Math: 550 / 640

Name:	Syracuse University
Location:	Syracuse, New York
Website:	www.syr.edu
US News & World 2012:	62 (tied)
QS Ranking 2012:	451-500
THE Ranking 2011-12:	not listed
Admission Profile:	Need-aware
Cost of attendance:	$60,150 (2012-2013)
Tuition element of cost:	$37,160
Admission rate:	43%
Admission deadline:	January 1
Scholarship deadline:	January 1
Common App®:	Yes
Advanced credit:	Higher IB

International student financial support:
International students are potentially eligible for two different types of financial support. SU anticipates international students will be fully funded but the Office of Admissions may invite students who have submitted the CSS Profile to apply for need-based aid. SU's International Applicant Form, detailing financial support available, must also be submitted in addition to the application for admission. Merit-based scholarships are awarded on the basis of exceptional academic and personal achievement. Selection is made by the Office of Admissions and eligibility is based on a student's academic credentials. Eligible students will be notified after they are admitted to Syracuse University.

Financial Documentation required
SU's international applicant form must be submitted in addition to the application for admission. Students must submit the CSS Profile if need-based aid is required.

Academic Merit Scholarships
There is no separate application process. Awards are made by the Admissions Committee and eligibility is based on a student's academic credentials, performance on standardised tests, class rank, portfolio or audition results (if relevant), community and extracurricular involvement and overall citizenship and character. Recipients must maintain a 2.75 GPA and complete at least 12 credits per semester. Awards: up to $12,000 per year and the number of awards vary.

Coronat Scholars
Students interested in a liberal arts major through The College of Arts and Sciences will be considered for the Coranat scholarship. In addition to an outstanding academic record, Coronat scholars are chosen on the basis of their records of leadership and service activities. Selected students will have achieved a combined SAT score of 1400 (Math and Critical Reasoning). Application is by invitation only.

and finalists will be interviewed on campus in March. Award: full tuition and funding for semester abroad. This scholarship is renewable.
The number of awards varies.

Freshman Profile Class of 2015

25th/ 75th Percentile

SAT Critical Reading 510 620

SAT Math 540 650

SAT Writing 520 630

ACT Composite 23 28

ACT Math 23 28

ACT English 23 28

ACT Writing 8 9

Name:	**Texas A&M University**
Location:	**College Station, Texas**
Website:	**www.tamu.edu**
US News & World 2012:	**58 (tied)**
QS Ranking 2012:	**165**
THE Ranking 2011-12:	**164**
Admission Profile:	No need-based aid, n/a
Cost of attendance:	$37,916 (2012-2013)
Tuition element of cost:	$24,919
Admission rate:	56%
Admission deadline:	January 15
Scholarship deadline:	n/a
Common App®:	No
Advanced credit:	Higher IB

International student financial support:
Texas A&M does not provide need-based financial aid to international students. Admitted students can apply for merit scholarships but awards are limited. Admitted international freshmen are required to show that they are able to support themselves for one year of attendance at Texas A&M. Continuing international students can apply for need-based aid and merit awards from their second year onwards.

Financial Documentation required
Proof of finances submitted after admission.

Merit awards for continuing international students
There are several merit-based scholarships open to international continuing students that range in value from $500 to $2,000. Most awards are single semester awards. There are no full or renewable scholarships.

Freshman Profile Class of 2015
Average SAT Score: 1220
Average ACT Score: 27

Name:	Texas Christian University
Location:	Fort Worth, Texas
Website:	www.tcu.edu
US News & World 2012:	97 (tied)
QS Ranking 2012:	not listed
THE Ranking 2011-12:	not listed
Admission Profile:	Need-aware
Cost of attendance:	$51,514 (2011-2012)
Tuition element of cost:	$34,500
Admission rate:	52%
Admission deadline:	March 1
Scholarship deadline:	December 15
Common App®:	Yes
Advanced credit:	Higher IB and A Level

International student financial support:

TCU offers both merit-based and need-based financial support to international students. TCU does not offer full funding awards so students should plan to be responsible for the majority of their educational expenses. All awards are competitive and usually cover less than half of the cost of attendance.

Financial Documentation required

TCU Financial Statement submitted as part of application for admission and students must submit the CSS Profile if requesting need-based aid.

Merit Scholarships

International applications that are received by December 15 are considered for TCU merit scholarships. There is no separate application process. Recipients will have strong high school grades and are required to submit SAT/ACT scores. Preferred scores for standardized tests are above 1800 on three sections of the SAT or 27+ on the ACT. Awards: from $3250 to $32,400 per year with a majority being under $14,000. Awards are renewable. The number of awards varies.

Freshman Profile Class of 2015

middle 50 percent scored:
between 1630 and 1900 on the SAT
between 24 and 29 on the ACT

Name:	**Tufts University**
Location:	**Medford, Massachusetts**
Website:	**www.tufts.edu**
US News & World 2012:	**29 (tied)**
QS Ranking 2012:	**181**
THE Ranking 2011-12:	77
Admission Profile:	Need-aware
Cost of attendance:	$58,800 (2012-2013)
Tuition element of cost:	$43,688
Admission rate:	22%
Admission deadline:	January 3
Scholarship deadline:	February 15 for need-based aid
Common App®:	Yes
Advanced credit:	Higher and Subsidiary Level IB, A Level

International student financial support:
Tufts has limited institutional resources (primarily grants) for aiding international students. While competition for international student financial aid is strong, the university is committed to maintaining and expanding its global campus community. The university awards financial aid only on the basis of demonstrated need. Tufts University does not offer any academic merit aid.

Applicants that will need financial aid at Tufts must apply for it when applying for admission. Financial aid is not available to international students who do not receive aid upon admittance. The family contribution determined upon acceptance will remain the same as long as the student is eligible to receive financial aid.

Financial Documentation required
CSS Profile on application if requesting need-based aid by February 15
International Student Certification of Finances ISFAA following admittance.

Freshman Profile Class of 2015
Mid-Range for SAT I Critical Reading 680-740
Mid-Range for SAT I Math 680-760
Mid-Range for SAT I Writing 680-760
Mean ACT Composite 31

Name:	Tulane University
Location:	New Orleans, Louisiana
Website:	www.tulane.edu
US News & World 2012:	50 (tied)
QS Ranking 2012:	309 (tied)
THE Ranking 2011-12:	201-250
Admission Profile:	Need sensitive
Cost of attendance:	$60,500 (2012-2013)
Tuition element of cost:	$45,240
Admission rate:	25%
Admission deadline:	January 15
	November 15 Early Action (non-binding)
Scholarship deadline:	January 15
	December 15 for Dean's Honors Scholarship
	and Global Scholarship
Common App®:	No
Advanced credit:	Higher IB and A Level

International student financial support:
Tulane offers both need-based and merit-based scholarships to international students. Need-based aid is limited to a maximum of $18,000 a year. Students who receive a merit-based scholarship in excess of this amount are not eligible for need-based aid. An international student and their family must expect to cover costs not covered by an award. All need-based scholarship recipients must maintain full-time enrolment (12 credit hours or more) each semester in a full-time division of Tulane (Newcomb- Tulane College, School of Architecture, School of Science and Engineering, School of Liberal Arts, Freeman School of Business). All admitted undergraduate students are considered for merit-based scholarships, and the review process is need-blind.

Financial Documentation required
Declaration and Certification of Finances submitted with application
CSS Profile for need-based aid must be submitted by February 15.

Merit-based Scholarships
All international freshmen applicants are considered for merit scholarships, which are awarded by the admission office based on superior academic record and extra-curricular activities. The Leadership Award, The Academic Achievement Award, The Founder's Scholarship, The Distinguished Scholar Award and The Presidential Scholarship do not require a separate application. Special application procedures and deadlines apply to the scholarships listed below.

Global Scholarship
See chapter six
Deans' Honor Scholarships
To be eligible applicants must submit their completed application for admission by the Early Action (non-binding) deadline and the Dean's Honor Scholarship application with teacher recommendation by December 15. Typical scholarship recipients rank in the top 5 percent, have a rigorous academic programme and have an outstanding record of extracurricular activities and excellent college admission test score. Application deadline: December 15. Award: full-tuition, renewable for 4 years, (or 5 years for Architecture) Number of awards: approx. 100 per year
Community Service Scholarship
The Tulane University Community Service Scholarship rewards students who have dedicated exceptional time and effort serving their communities and who plan to continue this dedication as members of the Tulane and New Orleans communities. Scholarship recipients will have to fulfill public service requirements each year for the scholarship to continue. These requirements are set by the Center for Public Service (CPS). Application deadline: January 15. Winners notified by April 1. Award: from $5,000 to $15,000, renewable for 4 years, (or 5 years for Architecture) Number of awards: limited
Freshman Profile Class of 2015
Middle 50%
SAT Composite 1950-2150
ACT Composite 29-32

Name:	The University of Alabama
Location:	Tuscaloosa, Alabama
Website:	www.ua.edu
US News & World 2012:	75 (tied)
QS Ranking 2012:	451-500
THE Ranking 2011-12:	not listed
Admission Profile:	No need-based aid, n/a
Cost of attendance:	$39,943 (2011-2012)
Tuition element of cost:	$21,900
Admission rate:	44%
Admission deadline:	March 1
	December 1 for merit scholarships
Scholarship deadline:	December 1
Common App®:	No
Advanced credit:	Higher IB

International student financial support:
UA does not provide need-based financial aid to international students. Admission will not be granted until the University has approved financial documentation. There are merit scholarships available to international students and these must be applied for online. UA requires that all freshman international students perform above the average. Students interested in applying must make contact with the International Undergraduate Admissions Office providing information on their educational background and degree interests. An application form will be mailed to qualified applicants.

Financial Documentation required
UA's Certification of Finances form submitted as part of application.

Merit Scholarships
To be considered for merit scholarships freshman applicants must submit both their complete admission application and the online scholarship application by December 1. They will then be considered for all the scholarships for which they are eligible. Grade point averages for years 10, 11 and 12 are the only years reviewed for scholarship consideration. October ACT and November SAT results are the last college entrance examination results accepted for students who wish to be considered for scholarships. Specific departmental merit scholarships are available in addition to those listed below that do not require a separate application; eligible applicants are considered automatically.

Capstone Scholar
An international freshman student who meets the December 1st scholarship priority deadline, has a 27 ACT or 1210-1240 SAT score (critical reading and math scores

only) and at least a 3.5 cumulative high-school GPA will be selected as a Capstone Scholar. Awards: $1,500 per year ($6,000 over four years)

Collegiate Scholar
An international freshman student who meets the December 1st scholarship priority deadline, has a 28-29 ACT or 1250-1320 SAT score [critical reading and math scores only] and at least a 3.5 cumulative hig-school GPA will be selected as a Collegiate Scholar. Awards: $3,500 per year ($14,000 over four years)

UA Scholar
An international freshman student who meets the December 1st scholarship priority deadline, has a 30-31 ACT or 1330-1390 SAT score (critical reading and math scores only) and at least a 3.5 cumulative high-school GPA will be selected as a UA Scholar. Awards are for 67% of the out-of-state tuition amount for four years

Presidential Scholar
An international freshman student who meets the December 1st scholarship priority deadline, has a 32-36 ACT or 1400-1600 SAT score (critical reading and math scores only) and at least a 3.5 cumulative high-school GPA will be selected as a Presidential Scholar. Award: out-of-state tuition cost for four years

Acadmic Elite Scholarships
To be considered for the Academic Elite Scholarships, a student must be accepted as a member of the University Fellows Experience (UFE). The student must maintain membership in the UFE to continue holding an Academic Elite Scholarship. A student with an ACT score of 32 or a SAT score of 1400 (critical reading and math scores only) and a high school GPA of 3.8 who is accepted into UA by the scholarship deadline of December 1 will be sent an application for the UFE. In the UFE selection process, the candidate's academic, extracurricular, service, and leadership achievements will weigh more heavily than grades and test scores. A student eligible for the University Honors Program (ACT of 28 or SAT of 1250) may be nominated for consideration for the Academic Elite Scholarships by a high school representative. The online nomination form (including the student's full contact information and letter of recommendation) must be completed by the high school representative by December 1.
Award: $8,500 per year for four years, value of tuition (in or out-of state), four years of on-campus housing and an iPad. Awards 8 to 10 per year.

Freshman Profile Class of 2015
25th /75th percentile

SAT Critical Reading 500/ 620	SAT Math 495 /640
SAT Writing 490 /610	ACT Composite 22 / 29

Name:	University of California, Berkeley
Location:	Berkeley, California
Website:	www.berkeley.edu
US News & World 2012:	20
QS Ranking 2012:	22
THE Ranking 2011-12:	10
Admission Profile:	No need-based aid, n/a
Cost of attendance:	$54,500 (2012-2013)
Tuition element of cost:	$37,400
Admission rate:	26%
Admission deadline:	30 November
Scholarship deadline:	November 30
Common App®:	No
Advanced credit:	Higher IB, A Level, subject to review.

International student financial support:
Berkeley does not provide need-based financial aid to international students. All admitted international students are required to show proof of funding for a minimum of one year with the expectation that students will continue to have access to that funding throughout their education. Individual departments at Berkeley may offer scholarships that are available to international students.

Students can apply to as many University of California undergraduate campuses as they like with just one online application, however, there is a separate fee for each application. Applications can only be submitted between November 1 and 30. Freshmen applicants must take the ACT with Writing or SAT Reasoning Test no later than December of their high school senior year. Students should have a report sent from the testing agency to one campus and it will be shared with all the campuses to which they apply. The application for admission includes scholarship applications for each campus but only a limited number are available to international students. Some campuses require additional supporting documents to be submitted in support of scholarship applications.

Financial Documentation required
Berkeley's Non-immigrant Information Form (NIF) is required. A guarantee by the applicant's financial sponsor proving sufficient funds for the first year of study is required.

The Leadership Award
The Leadership Award is a one-year, merit-based scholarship that recognises students who demonstrate innovative, motivational leadership impacting their academic, work, or community environments. Students compete for the scholarship every academic year.

International students are eligible to apply for this Award as incoming freshmen and in subsequent years at UCB. Having submitted an application to UCB in November students must submit the online application for the Leadership Award through the Cal Alumni Association UCB scholarship website. To be considered students must have a minimum high school GPA of 3.3, be available to interview in the US, London or Hong Kong, and submit a Statement of Intent to Register at Berkeley by May. Award: $2,000 for one year. The number of awards varies.

Freshman Profile Class of 2015

50% of enrolled students have test scores in the following ranges.

SAT Math 650-770

SAT Critical Reading 600-720

SAT Writing 620-740

Name:	University of California, Davis
Location:	Davis, California
Website:	www.ucdavis.edu
US News & World 2012:	38 (tied)
QS Ranking 2012:	100
THE Ranking 2011-12:	38
Admission Profile:	No need-based aid, n/a
Cost of attendance:	$54,500 (2012-2013)
Tuition element of cost:	$36,738
Admission rate:	46%
Admission deadline:	November 30
Scholarship deadline:	November 30
Common App®:	No
Advanced credit:	Higher IB

IB diploma students with a score of 30 or higher will receive 30 quarter (20 semester) units of credit toward an undergraduate degree

International student financial support:
UC Davis does not provide need-based financial aid to international students. International students are eligible for many UCD campus-based scholarships and will automatically be considered on the basis of their admissions application. Students can apply to as many University of California undergraduate campuses as they like with just one online application, however, there is a separate fee for each application. Applications can only be submitted between November 1 and 30. Freshmen applicants must take the ACT with Writing or SAT Reasoning Test no later than December of their high school senior year. Students should have a report sent from the testing agency to one campus and it will be shared with all the campuses to which they apply. The application for admission includes scholarship applications for each campus but only a limited number are available to international students. Some campuses require additional supporting documents to be submitted in support of scholarship applications.

Financial Documentation required
Proof of funds submitted after admission.

Regents' Scholarships
All applicants to UC Davis are considered for these awards, including international students. Awards are made on the basis of the information available in the student's UC Application for Undergraduate Admission, including GPA and SAT test scores. Other factors that may be considered include: the personal statement, extracurricular activities, academic potential, evidence of overcoming personal hardship, and other academic or personal qualities that will make a distinctive

contribution to the campus. The Regents Scholarship Advisory Committee reviews selection criteria annually. Award: $7,500 annually, renewable provided recipient maintains a cumulative 3.25 GPA. The number of awards varies.

Freshman Profile Class of 2015

Middle 50%

ACT Composite Score: 26-32

SAT Critical Reading: 550-690

SAT Mathematics: 610-740

Name:	University of California, Irvine
Location:	Irvine, California
Website:	www.uci.edu
US News & World 2012:	45 (tied)
QS Ranking 2012:	155
THE Ranking 2011-12:	86
Admission Profile:	No need-based aid, n/a
Cost of attendance:	$54,500 (2012-2013)
Tuition element of cost:	$36,916
Admission rate:	48%
Admission deadline:	November 30
Scholarship deadline:	November 30
Common App®:	No
Advanced credit:	Higher IB

International student financial support:
UC Irvine does not provide need-based financial aid to international students. .
Applicants are considered for merit-based campus scholarships on the basis of their
UC admissions application.

Students can apply to as many University of California undergraduate campuses as
they like with just one online application, however, there is a separate fee for each
application. Applications can only be submitted between November 1 and 30.
Freshmen applicants must take the ACT with Writing or SAT Reasoning exam no
later than December of their high school senior year. Students should have a report
sent from the testing agency to one campus and it will be shared with all the
campuses to which they apply. The application for admission includes scholarship
applications for each campus but only a limited number are available to
international students. Some campuses require additional supporting documents to
be submitted in support of scholarship applications.

Financial Documentation required
Bank statements are submitted after admission confirming sufficient funds are
available.

Henry Samueli Endowed Scholarship
This scholarship is awarded to outstanding freshmen students in The Henry
Samueli School of Engineering. Recipients are chosen by the school based on their
academic excellence. The award is renewable up to four years for freshmen. The UC
application for admission also serves as the application for this scholarship.

UCI Alumni Associate Scholarship
This merit-based scholarship is awarded to students who demonstrate academic
excellence, community service and leadership potential. Application is by invitation
only. After students submit their Statement of Intent to Register (SIR) by the

deadline, those who meet the qualifications will be invited to apply for the scholarship. Freshman applicants require a minimum GPA of 3.65. Eligible students will be notified via an e-mail that will include the application and information regarding the selection process.

Freshman Profile Class of 2015

Averages

ACT Composite Score: 27

SAT Critical Reading: 593

SAT Mathematics: 644

SAT Writing: 612

Name:	University of California, Los Angeles
Location:	Los Angeles, California
Website:	www.ucla.edu
US News & World 2012:	25 (tied)
QS Ranking 2012:	31
THE Ranking 2011-12:	13
Admission Profile:	No need-based aid, n/a
Cost of attendance:	$55,300 (2012-2013)
Tuition element of cost:	$36,540
Admission rate:	23%
Admission deadline:	30 November
Scholarship deadline:	n/a
Common App®:	No
Advanced credit:	Higher IB

International student financial support:

UCLA does not provide need-based or merit-based aid to international students. International students must prove that they have sufficient funds available to them to pay for their educational and living expenses.

Students can apply to as many University of California undergraduate campuses as they like with just one online application, however, there is a separate fee for each application. Applications can only be submitted between November 1 and 30. Freshmen applicants must take the ACT with Writing or SAT Reasoning exam no later than December of their high school senior year. Students should have a report sent from the testing agency to one campus and it will be shared with all the campuses to which they apply.

Financial Documentation required

Proof of finances submitted after admission.

Freshman Profile Class of 2015

Averages: ACT Composite Score: 30

SAT Critical Reading: 657

SAT Mathematics: 701

SAT Writing: 680

Name:	University of California, Riverside
Location:	Riverside, California
Website:	www.ucr.edu
US News & World 2012:	97 (tied)
QS Ranking 2012:	303
THE Ranking 2011-12:	143
Admission Profile:	No need-based aid, n/a
Cost of attendance:	$54,500 (2012-2013)
Tuition element of cost:	$36,540
Admission rate:	69%
Admission deadline:	November 30
Scholarship deadline:	November 30
Common App®:	No
Advanced credit:	Higher IB and A Level
	IB diploma students with a score of 30 or above will receive 30 quarter units (20 semester units) total toward their UCR undergraduate degree.

International student financial support:
UC Riverside does not provide need-based financial aid to international students. Merit-based scholarships are limited.
Students can apply to as many University of California undergraduate campuses as they like with just one online application, however, there is a separate fee for each application. Applications can only be submitted between November 1 and 30. Freshmen applicants must take the ACT with Writing or SAT Reasoning exam no later than December of their high school senior year. Students should have a report sent from the testing agency to one campus and it will be shared with all the campuses to which they apply. The application for admission includes scholarship applications for each campus but only a limited number are available to international students. Some campuses require additional supporting documents to be submitted in support of scholarship applications.
Financial Documentation required
Proof of finances submitted after admission.
Regents' Scholarships
The Regents' Scholarship is the most prestigious scholarship awarded to incoming UCR freshmen. Students are selected based on a review of the academic record by the faculty Committee on Scholarships and Honors. New Regents Scholars are notified of the award at the time of admission. Regents Scholarships will be awarded to students for up to four years if all renewal criteria are met.

145

Chancellor's Scholarship

The Chancellor's Scholarship is a merit based award offered to incoming UCR freshmen with a distinguished academic record. The Chancellor's Scholarship provides an honorarium applied toward fees.

Alumni Scholarships

The Alumni Association awards merit-based scholarships to freshmen each year. During the 2012-13 academic year, 12 incoming freshmen will each be awarded a $4,000 scholarship. Applicants must be incoming freshman attending UCR in the fall and have a minimum high-school GPA of 3.5. SAT scores must also be included.

Freshman Profile Class of 2015

ACT Composite Score: 25
SAT Critical Reading: 551
SAT Mathematics: 595

Name:	University of California, San Diego
Location:	La Jolla, California
Website:	www.ucsd.edu
US News & World 2012:	37
QS Ranking 2012:	70
THE Ranking 2011-12:	33
Admission Profile:	No need-based aid, n/a
Cost of attendance:	$54,500 (2012-2013)
Tuition element of cost:	$35,900
Admission rate:	35%
Admission deadline:	November 30
Scholarship deadline:	n/a
Common App®:	No
Advanced credit:	Higher IB

International student financial support:
UCSD does not offer need-based or merit based financial aid to international students.

Students can apply to as many University of California undergraduate campuses as they like with just one online application, however, there is a separate fee for each application. Applications can only be submitted between November 1 and 30. Freshmen applicants must take the ACT with Writing or SAT Reasoning exam no later than December of their high school senior year. Students should have a report sent from the testing agency to one campus and it will be shared with all the campuses to which they apply.

Financial Documentation required
Proof of finances submitted after admission and when confirming enrolment.

Freshman Profile Class of 2015
Averages
ACT Composite Score: 29
SAT Critical Reading: 632
SAT Mathematics: 681
SAT Writing: 653

Name:	**University of California, Santa Barbara**
Location:	**Santa Barbara, California**
Website:	**www.ucsb.edu**
US News & World 2012:	**42 (tied)**
QS Ranking 2012:	**118**
THE Ranking 2011-12:	**35**
Admission Profile:	No need-based aid, n/a
Cost of attendance:	$55,254 (2012-2013)
Tuition element of cost:	$37,800
Admission rate:	46%
Admission deadline:	30 November
Scholarship deadline:	n/a
Common App®:	No
Advanced credit:	Higher IB and A Level

International student financial support:

UC Santa Barbara does not provide need-based financial aid to international students. The application for admission includes scholarship applications for each campus but only a limited number are available to international students. Students can apply to as many University of California undergraduate campuses as they like with just one online application, however, there is a separate fee for each application. Applications can only be submitted between November 1 and 30. Freshmen applicants must take the ACT with Writing or SAT Reasoning exam no later than December of their high school senior year. Students should have a report sent from the testing agency to one campus and it will be shared with all the campuses to which they apply.

Financial Documentation required

UCSB's financial statement for admitted international students and proof of finances must be submitted after admission when student submits the Statement of Intent to Register (SIR).

Global Excellence Scholarships

The University of California at Santa Barbara has established The Global Scholarship for freshman applicants who live outside California. The prestigious merit-based award will recognize the academic achievements of top non-resident freshmen who are offered admission to UCSB. Students will not apply for the Global Scholarship; eligibility will be calculated automatically as part of the admission process. Award: $20,000 over four years. The number of awards varies.

Freshman Profile Class of 2015

Average ACT Composite Score: 28
Average SAT Critical Reading: 613, SAT Math: 647, SAT Writing: 62

Name:	University of California, Santa Cruz
Location:	Santa Cruz, California
Website:	www.ucsc.edu
US News & World 2012:	75 (tied)
QS Ranking 2012:	311
THE Ranking 2011-12:	110
Admission Profile:	No need-based aid, n/a
Cost of attendance:	$56,301 (2012-2013)
Tuition element of cost:	$37,974
Admission rate:	68%
Admission deadline:	30 November
Scholarship deadline:	30 November
Common App®:	No
Advanced credit:	Higher IB
	Full IB Diploma score of 30 and above will receive 30 credits

International student financial support:

UCSC does not offer need-based financial support to international students. International freshman applicants are encouraged to complete the scholarship section of the admission application.

Students can apply to as many University of California undergraduate campuses as they like with just one online application, however, there is a separate fee for each application. Applications can only be submitted between November 1 and 30. Freshmen applicants must take the ACT with Writing or SAT Reasoning exam no later than December of their high school senior year. Students should have a report sent from the testing agency to one campus and it will be shared with all the campuses to which they apply.

Financial Documentation required

UCSC's Confidential Financial Certificate submitted with supporting documents after admission.

Undergraduate Dean's Award

This award recognizes the academic achievement of non-resident students, including international students. Selection criteria vary from year to year depending upon the applicant pool. Award: $4,000 for the first and second years, $6,000 for the third and fourth years; recipients must remain full-time and maintain a 3.0 GPA The number of awards varies.

Freshman Profile Class of 2015

Average ACT Composite Score: 26

Average SAT Critical Reading: 580

Average SAT Mathematics: 605

Name:	The University of Chicago
Location:	Chicago, Illinois
Website:	www.uchicago.edu
US News & World 2012:	5 (tied)
QS Ranking 2012:	8
THE Ranking 2011-12:	9
Admission Profile:	Need-aware
Cost of attendance:	$62,425 (2012-2013)
Tuition element of cost:	$43,581
Admission rate:	16%
Admission deadline:	January 1
Scholarship deadline:	January 1
Common App®:	Yes
Advanced credit:	Higher IB and A Level

International student financial support:

University of Chicago takes into account whether or not an international applicant has requested financial assistance. The UChicago will meet every admitted student's demonstrated need but has a limited fund for international students. UChicago advises international students to apply for financial aid only if they do not have the resources to fund their education, and to complete the financial aid form as accurately as possible. Students who apply for financial aid and are admitted will receive a financial award in the form of grants and scholarships.

International students are only eligible for financial aid if they apply for support during the admissions process.

Financial Documentation required

International Student Financial Aid Application and supporting documents submitted to the University by January 1 if applying for need-based aid.

Merit Scholarships

Merit scholarships are awarded to applicants on the basis of outstanding academic and extracurricular achievement, demonstrated leadership, and commitment to their communities. Merit awards are determined by Faculty Committee and the Office of College Admissions without consideration of financial need, and are guaranteed for four years of undergraduate study.

To be considered for a merit scholarship check the box on the Common Application. All first-year applicants are eligible.

Freshman Profile Class of 2015

ACT Middle 50% 31–34	ACT Score Range 23–36
SAT Middle 50% 1420–1530	SAT Score Range 1100–1600

Name:	University of Colorado-Boulder
Location:	Boulder, Colorado
Website:	www.colorado.edu
US News & World 2012:	94 (tied)
QS Ranking 2012:	157
THE Ranking 2011-12:	77
Admission Profile:	No need-based aid, n/a
Cost of attendance:	$44,560 (2012-2013)
Tuition element of cost:	$30,330
Admission rate:	87%
Admission deadline:	January 15
Scholarship deadline:	January 15
Common App®:	No
Advanced credit:	Higher IB

Admitted students who graduated from high school with an IB Diploma shall be granted 24 semester hours of college credit.

International student financial support:
CU-Boulder does not provide need-based financial aid to international students. There are merit scholarships open to international students but funds are limited and highly competitive. CU-Boulder offers international students a guaranteed four-year tuition promise, which means that the cost of tuition will be constant for the four full years. SAT/ACT tests are optional for international students unless they want merit scholarship consideration.

Financial Documentation required
Financial Statement for International Applicants required before admission finalized but application can be reviewed before submission of proof of funding.

Automatic Consideration Scholarships
International freshmen applicants are automatically considered for merit scholarships based on the strength of their admissions application, high school record and their SAT/ACT scores. Generally this means having a high school GPA of 3.8 or higher, a SAT score above 1270 (Math and Critical Reading) or an ACT score of 30 or above. No separate application is required

The Chancellor's Achievement Scholarship
Available to out-of-state and international students who are in the top 25% academically of the admitted non-US resident class at CU-Boulder. Award: $20,000 over four years. The number of awards varies.

Presidential Scholarship Program
Each year, about 10% of Chancellor's Achievement Scholars receive The Presidential Scholarship for academic achievement at the high school level. If selected to receive

the Presidential Scholarship, students are not eligible to receive the Chancellor's Achievement Scholarship. Award: $55,000 over four years.
The number of awards varies.

Norlin Scholars

Norlin Scholar applicants must submit a separate application and can submit it as soon as they have applied to CU-Boulder. They do not need to be admitted first. Candidates demonstrate strong academic commitment, exceptional creativity, intellectual curiosity and a desire to apply disciplinary learning toward the betterment of humanity. Awards are renewable for up to four years providing the recipient is maintaining a minimum 3.25 GPA, progressing towards specific Norlin programme requirements, is participating in the scholar community, and adhering to CU's professional, academic and personal codes of conduct.

Award: $4000, application deadline is February 15. The number of awards varies.

Freshman Profile Class of 2015

Middle 50%

SAT 1080–1270 (Math and Critical Reading)

ACT 24–29

Name:	**University of Connecticut**
Location:	**Storrs, Connecticut**
Website:	**www.uconn.edu**
US News & World 2012:	**58 (tied)**
QS Ranking 2012:	**366**
THE Ranking 2011-12:	**not listed**
Admission Profile:	No need-based aid, n/a
Cost of attendance:	$45,880 (2012-2013)
Tuition element of cost:	$26,554
Admission rate:	47%
Admission deadline:	January 15
Scholarship deadline:	n/a
Common App®:	Yes
Advanced credit:	Higher IB - limited subjects

International student financial support:
UConn does not provide need-based or merit-based financial aid to international students.

Financial Documentation required
International Undergraduate Student Financial Declaration Form submitted after admission. Sponsor has to submit Affidavit of Support - if they live outside the United States, the affidavit must be sworn to or affirmed before a U.S. consular or immigration officer.

Freshman Profile Class of 2015
Average SAT score: 1216 (Critical Reading and Math)

Name:	**University of Delaware**
Location:	**Newark, Delaware**
Website:	**www.udel.edu**
US News & World 2012:	**75 (tied)**
QS Ranking 2012:	**401-450**
THE Ranking 2011-12:	**180**
Admission Profile:	No need-based aid, n/a
Cost of attendance:	$42,500 (2012-2013)
Tuition element of cost:	$26,725
Admission rate:	58%
Admission deadline:	January 15
Scholarship deadline:	December 1
Common App®:	Yes
Advanced credit:	Higher IB

International student financial support:
UD does not provide need-based financial aid to international students. International freshman applicants applying for fall admission will automatically be considered for merit scholarships provided they meet the priority admissions application deadline of December 1

Financial Documentation required
UD's confidential financial Information form is due by mail at time of application.

Merit Scholarships
Unless contacted by UD for additional information, students do not have to submit a separate application for merit scholarships. All applications are considered and awards are made on the basis of the strength and excellence of the high school record. Outstanding out-of-class accomplishments and leadership, strong endorsements in letters of recommendation, a background or heritage that would lend diversity to the campus, a parent who is an alumnus/a of the University, and exceptionally strong writing samples also play a part in scholarship decisions.

Eugene DuPont Memorial Distinguished Scholar Awards
This is the UD's most prestigious merit scholarship.
Award: full tuition, room and board, books. Number of awards: 10-12 per year

Freshman Profile Class of 2015
Middle 50% of admitted freshmen SAT I: 1780-2000
Middle 50% of freshmen SAT I in Honours Program 2030-2200
Average freshmen ACT Composite 27, Average Honors Program ACT: 31.

Name:	University of Denver
Location:	Denver, Colorado
Website:	www.du.edu
US News & World 2012:	82 (tied)
QS Ranking 2012:	601+
THE Ranking 2011-12:	not listed
Admission Profile:	No need-based aid, n/a
Cost of attendance:	$57,996 (2012-2013)
Tuition element of cost:	$38,232
Admission rate:	72%
Admission deadline:	January 15
Scholarship deadline:	January 15
Common App®:	Yes
Advanced credit:	Higher IB

International student financial support:
DU does not provide need-based financial aid to international students. The University of Denver's commitment to international students and scholastic excellence is exemplified by a number of merit-based scholarships awarded to new first-year international students annually. All qualified applicants are given automatic consideration for these scholarships; there is no separate application. SAT or ACT results and class rankings are used to determine eligibility for merit-based awards. Priority consideration for admission is given to international students who submit proof of finances with their admission application. There are no full-tuition scholarships and awards are for partial tuition at varying rates. Priority admission review will be given to those who submit proof of finances with their application.

Financial Documentation required
Financial Verification Form for international students required after admission but priority consideration given to applicants that verify funds at time of application.

Merit-based Scholarships
Admitted students have typically earned the equivalent of A's and B's in a demanding, college preparatory curriculum. Award: from $10,000 to $ 19,000 per year, renewable.

Music Activity Scholarship
All DU music scholarships are very competitive and are reserved for the very best applicants. The awards are based on the quality of the audition, portfolio or interview, and proven potential for future success. All of those who pass a successful audition will automatically be considered for a music scholarship. There is no additional application necessary. Award: from $1,000 to full tuition, renewable.

Freshman Profile Class of 2015

Test Score Ranges (Mid 50%)

Scores for the following tests are represented as low | average | high

SAT I Verbal: 540 | 595 | 650

SAT I Math: 560 | 610 | 660

SAT Combined: 1,640|1,797 | 1,955

ACT English: 25 | 28 | 32

ACT Math: 24 | 26 | 29

ACT Composite: 25 | 27 | 30

Name:	University of Florida
Location:	Gainesville, Florida
Website:	www.ufl.edu
US News & World 2012:	58 (tied)
QS Ranking 2012:	169
THE Ranking 2011-12:	125
Admission Profile:	No need-based aid, n/a
Cost of attendance:	$43,700 (2012-2013)
Tuition element of cost:	$28,448
Admission rate:	43%
Admission deadline:	November 1
Scholarship deadline:	n/a
Common App®:	No
Advanced credit:	IB

International student financial support:
UF does not provide need-based or merit-based financial aid to international students.

Financial Documentation required
Certificate of Financial Responsibility and proof of funds submitted after admission.

Freshman Profile Class of 2015
Middle 50% of the Class
SAT of 1830-2090
ACT of 28 – 32

Name:	The University of Georgia
Location:	Athens, Georgia
Website:	www.uga.edu
US News & World 2012:	62 (tied)
QS Ranking 2012:	387
THE Ranking 2011-12:	201-225
Admission Profile:	No need-based aid, n/a
Cost of attendance:	$41,303 (2011-2012)
Tuition element of cost:	$28,500
Admission rate:	63%
Admission deadline:	January 15 unless applying for scholarships
Scholarship deadline:	November 1 for Foundation Fellowship and Bernard Ramsey Honors
	December 15 all other merit scholarships
Common App®:	No
Advanced credit:	Standard and Higher IB

International student financial support:
UGA does not provide need-based financial aid to international students. Students are expected to be self-supported. International students are considered for merit scholarships.

Financial Documentation required
UGA Certificate of Finances and supporting documents submitted as part of application for admission.

Foundation Fellowship
Recipients have a record of strong academic achievement and a history of accomplishment and leadership in co-curricular activities, a minimum GPA of 3.75 and a minimum 1400 SAT (on critical reading and math only, writing score required) or 31 ACT is necessary. Award: $15,700 annual stipend for out-of-state students (in addition to a Regents Out-of-State tuition waiver). Awards: 18-22.

Bernard Ramsey Honors Scholarship
Recipients have a record of strong academic achievement and a history of accomplishment and leadership in co-curricular activities. Scores necessary include a minimum academic GPA of 3.75 and a minimum 1400 SAT (on critical reading and math only; writing score required) or 31 ACT.
Award: $7,700 annual stipend for out-of-state students (in addition to a Regents out-of-state tuition waiver). Number of awards: 25-30

Presidential Scholarship
Recipients have a record of strong academic achievement and a history of accomplishment and leadership in co-curricular activities.

Award: $3,000 annual stipend for out-of-state students (in addition to a Regents out-of-state tuition waiver). Number of awards: 40-45

George Woodruff Scholarship

Recipients have a record of strong academic achievement and who will enrol in the Honors Program will be considered.
Award: $2,000 annually. Number of awards: 2-3

Dr. Henry King Stanford Scholarship

Recipients have a record of strong academic achievement and a history of accomplishment and leadership in co-curricular activities. Only students who have applied for the Foundation Fellowship and enrol in the Honors Program will be considered for the Henry King Stanford Scholarship. Scores necessary include a minimum academic GPA of 3.70 and a minimum 1400 SAT (on critical reading and math only; writing score required) or 31 ACT. Award: $3,000 annual stipend for out-of-state students (in addition to a Regents Out-of-State Tuition Waiver). Number of awards: 2-3.

Regents Waivers

Awarded in conjunction with other University merit scholarships. Waives half or all of the difference between in-state and out-of-state tuition.
Number of awards: 75-100.

Freshman Profile Class of 2015

25th Percentile 75th Percentile
SAT Critical Reading 560 650
SAT Math 560 660
SAT Writing 560 650
ACT Composite 25 30
ACT Math 25 29
ACT English 25 31
ACT Writing 7 9

Name:	University of Illinois at Urbana-Champaign
Location:	Urbana-Champaign, Illinois
Website:	www.uiuc.edu
US News & World 2012:	45 (tied)
QS Ranking 2012:	56
THE Ranking 2011-12:	31
Admission Profile:	No need-based aid, n/a
Cost of attendance:	$54,300 (2012-2013)
Tuition element of cost:	$36,822
Admission rate:	69%
Admission deadline:	January 1
	Priority Filing November 1
Scholarship deadline:	January 1
	Priority Scholarships November 1
Common App®:	No
Advanced credit:	Higher and subsidiary IB and A Level

International student financial support:

The University of Illinois does not provide need-based financial aid to international students. Merit-based scholarships are limited. Financial verification is not required until students are admitted. The Undergraduate Application for Admission is used for all merit-based scholarships. Applicants are automatically considered for scholarships. Priority for scholarships may be given to applicants who apply during the priority filing period. Scholarships are granted based on academic achievement and are awarded by individual colleges and departments.

Financial Documentation required

Proof of finances submitted after admission.

University Achievement Scholarship

Awarded to out-of-state incoming freshmen with outstanding academic achievement. Award: $12,000 renewable for four years, provided the student maintains a 3.0 GPA. The number of awards varies.

Freshman Profile Class of 2015

25th Percentile 75th Percentile scores:

SAT Critical Reading 540 660   SAT Math 690 780   SAT Writing 590 680
ACT Composite 26 31   ACT Math 26 33   ACT English 26 32
ACT Writing 25 30

Name:	The University of Iowa
Location:	Iowa City, Iowa
Website:	www.uiowa.edu
US News & World 2012:	71 (tied)
QS Ranking 2012:	199
THE Ranking 2011-12:	141
Admission Profile:	No need-based aid, n/a
Cost of attendance:	$39,725 (2012-2013)
Tuition element of cost:	$24,900
Admission rate:	84%
Admission deadline:	March 1 (Pharmacy is January 1)
Scholarship deadline:	varies by scholarship
Common App®:	No
Advanced credit:	Higher IB (also Subsidiary level Mathematics)

International student financial support:
The University of Iowa does not provide need-based financial aid to international students. Iowa offers several scholarships to outstanding international first-year students.

Financial Documentation required
Iowa's Financial Statement for International Applicants must be submitted once admitted.

Presidential and the Old Gold Scholarships
Scholarship recipients require an ACT composite score of 30 or above or a combined SAT critical reading and math score of 1330 or above AND a cumulative high school grade-point average (GPA) of 3.80 or above on a 4.00 scale. Both scholarships require the same application and supporting materials which have to be submitted in December. The top 20 candidates are awarded the Presidential Scholarship and the Old Gold Scholarship. Up to 350 of the next tier of applicants are awarded the Old Gold Scholarship.
Award: $13,000 per year for the combined award, renewable; $3,000 for the Old Gold. Number of awards: 20 Presidential and Old Gold combined; up to 350 Old Gold only, renewable.

Dean Gerhard Loewenberg Scholarship
Awarded to the top ranking alternate in the Presidential Scholarship competition. Student must be majoring in College of Liberal Arts and Sciences programmes only. Award: $1000 to $2500, non-renewable. Number of awards: one.

College of Liberal Arts and Sciences Excellence Award
A one-time award to selected first-year Old Gold Scholars with majors in the College of Liberal Arts and Sciences. Award: $1,000-2,000.
Number of awards: up to five per year.

University of Iowa International Scholars Award (ISA)

International first-year students with outstanding high school records are considered automatically upon admission. The ISA award is based on a review of student's high school record including high school courses, course rigor, and grades earned in those courses. Award: $2,000, renewable. The number of awards varies.

Iowa Heritage Award

For entering international students who have a parent, stepparent, legal guardian, or grandparent who graduated from The University of Iowa with a Bachelor's, Master's, or Doctoral degree. Application is due May 1.
Award: $1,500, renewable.

India Scholars Award

International first-year students whose country of citizenship is India are considered automatically upon admission. The India Scholars Award will be awarded at the time of admission to students with outstanding high school records including high school courses, course rigor, and grades earned in those courses.
Award: $1,500 a year, renewable.

Tippie Scholars Scholarships

International students who qualify for direct admission to the Tippie School of Business as freshman can apply for the highly competive Tippie Scholars Scholarship. Awards are based on academic merit and the application essay.
Award: $1,500-$2,500, one-time award.   Number of awards: up to 30.

Freshman Profile Class of 2015

Middle 50%
ACT composite 23-28
SAT (combined Critical Reading + Math) 1060-1260

Name:	University of Maryland
Location:	College Park, Maryland
Website:	www.umd.edu
US News & World 2012:	55 (tied)
QS Ranking 2012:	117
THE Ranking 2011-12:	94
Admission Profile:	No need-based aid, n/a
Cost of attendance:	$45,526 (2011-2012)
Tuition element of cost:	$26,026
Admission rate:	42%
Admission deadline:	January 20
	November 1 for best consideration
Scholarship deadline:	n/a
Common App®:	No
Advanced credit:	Higher IB and A Level

International student financial support:
The University of Maryland does not provide merit or need-based financial aid to international students.

Financial Documentation required
Certification of Finances submitted with application for admission.

Freshman Profile Class of 2016
Middle 50% of SAT 1250 to 1400
ACT between 28-32

Name:	University of Massachusetts Amherst
Location:	Amherst, Massachusetts
Website:	www.umass.edu
US News & World 2012:	94 (tied)
QS Ranking 2012:	255
THE Ranking 2011-12:	64
Admission Profile:	No need-based aid, n/a
Cost of attendance:	$46,600 (2012-2013)
Tuition element of cost:	$26,650
Admission rate:	68%
Admission deadline:	January 15
Scholarship deadline:	n/a
Common App®:	Yes
Advanced credit:	Higher IB and A Level

International student financial support:
UMass does not provide need-based or merit-based financial aid to international students.

Financial Documentation required
Undergraduate Sponsor Statement can be submitted after admission.

Freshman Profile Class of 2014
Test Score Ranges (Mid 50%)
Scores for the following tests are represented as low score | average score | high score
SAT I Verbal: 520 | 570 | 620
SAT I Math: 540 | 590 | 640
SAT Combined: 1,580 | 1,730 | 1,880
ACT Composite: 23 | 25 | 28

Name:	University of Miami
Location:	Coral Gables, Florida
Website:	www.miami.edu
US News & World 2012:	38 (tied)
QS Ranking 2012:	231
THE Ranking 2011-12:	172
Admission Profile:	No need-based aid, n/a
Cost of attendance:	$60,288 (2012-2013)
Tuition element of cost:	$39,980
Admission rate:	39%
Admission deadline:	January 1
	December 1 for Frost School of Music
Scholarship deadline:	January 1
	December 1 for Music
Common App®:	Yes
Advanced credit:	Higher Level IB

International student financial support:
UM does not provide need-based financial aid to international students. International applicants are eligible for competitive merit-based/academic scholarships. All admitted applicants are considered for merit scholarships provided they meet the minimum combined SAT score of 1300 (critical reading and math).

Financial Documentation required
Bank letter confirming funds submitted as part of the admission application.

Academic Scholarships for International Freshmen students
When selecting students for academic scholarships, UM takes into account the student's high school curriculum, difficulty of course selection (such as AP/IB), extracurricular activities, essay and letter(s) of recommendation, as well as the overall quality of the students applying. There is no other separate application process. International applicants studying outside the USA should only submit their SAT scores if they qualify for merit scholarship consideration. Frost School of Music students will be considered for University of Miami scholarships based on music talent and academic performance. The maximum award is equal to full tuition. Merit scholarships are renewable provided that students maintain a 3.0 GPA and attend full-time (minimum 24 credit hours per academic year).

To be considered for a merit scholarship, international candidates must also submit a complete application for admission with all academic credentials and a bank letter by the application deadline. The bank letter must confirm that the applicant will be able to cover the difference between the scholarship award and the total cost of attendance (approximately $19,000).

Isaac Bashevis Singer Scholarship
Minimum criteria: Top 1% class rank; SAT 1500 or ACT 34
Award: full tuition.
University Scholarship
Minimum criteria: Top 1% class rank; SAT 1450 or ACT 33
Award: $24,000 annually.
Dickinson Scholarship
Minimum criteria: Top 5% class rank; SAT 1350 or ACT 31
Award: $20,000 annually.
Dean's Scholarship
Minimum criteria: Top 10% class rank; SAT 1300 or ACT 30
Award: $10,000 annually.
Freshman Profile Class of 2015
Mid-range SAT scores (Math & Verbal)
25th / 75th Percentile 1270 / 1400
Mid-range ACT scores
25th /75th Percentile 29/ 32

Name:	University of Michigan, Ann Arbor
Location:	Ann Arbor, Michigan
Website:	www.umich.edu
US News & World 2012:	28
QS Ranking 2012:	17
THE Ranking 2011-12:	18
Admission Profile:	No need-based aid, n/a
Cost of attendance:	$53,006 (2012-2013)
Tuition element of cost:	$37,782
Admission rate:	40%
Admission deadline:	February 1
Scholarship deadline:	n/a
Common App®:	Yes
Advanced credit:	Higher IB, A Level
	Cambridge Pre-U (excluding GPR)

International student financial support:
University of Michigan does not provide need-based or merit-based financial aid to international students.

Financial Documentation required
U-M's Financial Resources Statement submitted after admission.

Freshman Profile Class of 2015
Middle 50th Percentile
ACT Composite of 29-33
ACT English of 29-34
ACT Math of 28-34
ACT Science 27-33
ACT Combined English/Writing of 27-31
SAT Total of 1990-2200
SAT Critical Reading 630-730
SAT Math 670-770
SAT Writing 650-750
AP and/or IB credit was granted to over 3,000 new freshmen

Name:	University of Minnesota, Twin Cities
Location:	Minneapolis, Minnesota
Website:	www.umn.edu
US News & World 2012:	68 (tied)
QS Ranking 2012:	104
THE Ranking 2011-12:	42
Admission Profile:	No need-based aid, n/a
Cost of attendance:	$35,075 (2012-2013)
Tuition element of cost:	$19,336
Admission rate:	76%
Admission deadline:	December 15
Scholarship deadline:	December 15
Common App®:	No
Advanced credit:	Higher IB

International student financial support:
The University of Minnesota does not provide need-based financial aid to international students. The University of Minnesota offers a limited number of Global Excellence Scholarships for incoming international freshmen.

Financial Documentation required
UM's Financial Certification Statement submitted after admission.

Global Excellence Scholarships
All international incoming freshman and transfer students are eligible for the Global Excellence Scholarship. Students are considered for these awards based on an overall assessment of the admission application. A formal application is not required. Award: from $2500 to $5000 towards tuition costs per year, renewable.

Freshman Profile Class of 2015
25th Percentile 75th Percentile
SAT Critical Reading 450 580
SAT Math 480 610
SAT Writing 470 590
ACT Composite 22 26
ACT Math 22 26
ACT English 20 25
ACT Writing 6 8

Name:	University of Missouri
Location:	Columbia, Missouri
Website:	www.missouri.edu
US News & World 2012:	90 (tied)
QS Ranking 2012:	385 (tied)
THE Ranking 2011-12:	226-250
Admission Profile:	No need-based aid, n/a
Cost of attendance:	$32,571 (2011-2012)
Tuition element of cost:	$16,566
Admission rate:	82%
Admission deadline:	February 1
	December 1 for merit scholarship
	consideration
Scholarship deadline:	December 1
Common App®:	No
Advanced credit:	Higher and Subsidiary IB

International student financial support:

MU does not provide need-based financial aid to international students. Merit-based financial aid resources for international students are highly competitive.

Financial Documentation required

Affidavit of Support is part of international undergraduate student application.

International Merit Scholarship

All eligible admitted students will be considered. There is no separate application. To be considered students must have a combined SAT score of 1200 or higher (critical reading and math scores) and a minimum TOEFL score of 79 or higher (550-pbt; or 7.0 IELTS overall band score). Award: $4,000 per year, renewable for a total of 8 semesters provided student maintains a 3.25 GPA. The number of awards varies.

Global Heritage Award

In addition to having a parent who graduated from MU, recipients must have a combined SAT I minimum score of 1200 (critical reading and math scores) or a minimum composite ACT score of 27 to be eligible. Application required. Award: Non-resident tuition waiver, renewable for a total of 8 semesters provided student maintains a minimum cumulative 3.25 GPA. The number of awards varies.

Freshman Profile Class of 2015

25/ 75 Percentile

SAT Critical Reading 530 650	SAT Math 520 650
ACT Composite 23 28	ACT Math 22 27

Name:	**The University of North Carolina**
Location:	**Chapel Hill, North Carolina**
Website:	**www.unc.edu**
US News & World 2012:	**29 (tied)**
QS Ranking 2012:	**57**
THE Ranking 2011-12:	**43**
Admission Profile:	No need-based aid, n/a
Cost of attendance:	$46,080 (2012-2013)
Tuition element of cost:	$29,515
Admission rate:	31%
Admission deadline:	January 5
Scholarship deadline:	January 5 for UNC merit scholarships
Common App®:	Yes
Advanced credit:	Higher IB
	Subsidiary IB for languages
	A Level

International student financial support:

UNC does not provide need-based financial aid to international students and international students should be prepared to pay the full cost of attendance for non-resident students. International students are considered for a very limited number of merit scholarships. There is no separate application for these scholarships. Awards are made to students who demonstrate outstanding academic achievement, strong curiosity and leadership skills.

Financial Documentation required

UNC's Financial Certificate for International Applicants and supporting documents submitted after admission.

The Scholars Program

Criteria for The Scholars Program merit-based scholarships include academic achievement, leadership qualities, commitment to service, and potential for success at the University. The University seeks to identify students who have earned academic distinction in high school, but selection goes beyond metrics of test scores and grade point averages, focusing on a holistic review of the entire application.

The Scholars Program at Carolina is made up of the Carolina Scholars, Colonel Robinson Scholars, Pogue Scholars and Johnston Scholars. International students are not considered for the Johnston Scholars Program. There is no separate application and selection is based on the information provided in the application for admission. Competition is very strong.

Number of awards: Approximately 200 merit scholarships are awarded each year to the incoming class.

Carolina Scholars

The Carolina Scholars programme is designed to attract the most promising high school students to the University of North Carolina at Chapel Hill. The programme seeks to identify talented freshmen, enrich their academic experience, and encourage their contributions to the intellectual life of the University. Award: tuition, fees, room and board for international students. Renewable for 8 semesters provided scholars maintain a 3.0 GPA

Colonel Robinson Scholars

This scholarship is geared toward students studying science, maths and technology. Award: : tuition, fees, room and board for international students. Renewable for 8 semesters maintaining 3.0 GPA. For the Carolina and Colonel Robinson Scholarships, candidates are selected on the basis of their admissions applications and are invited to attend one of two Scholar Day events held at the University in the Spring. During Scholar Day, determinations are made regarding which candidates will be offered a scholarship and in what amount.

Pogue Scholarships

The Pogue Scholarship Program seeks to identify students who demonstrate academic achievement, commitment to community service and exhibit strong leadership potential. The Pogue Scholarship Program believes that diversity extends beyond race and ethnicity to include consideration of students' personal backgrounds and life experiences. Students who represent the first generation of their family to pursue post-secondary education are particularly encouraged to apply. To be considered for the Pogue Scholarship students must submit their application to UNC by October 15. Candidates are selected on the basis of their admissions applications, and then invited to submit additional information that will be reviewed by the Pogue Scholarship Selection Committee. Finalists will be invited to Chapel Hill for a two-day event that includes an interview. Award: tuition, fees, room and board for international students. Renewable for 8 semesters provided Scholars retain a 3.0 GPA.

Robertson Scholars Program

See chapter five

Morehead-Cain Scholarship

See chapter five

Freshman Profile Class of 2015

25th-75th percentiles

SAT Critical Reading 590-700	SAT Math 610-710
SAT Writing 610-690	ACT Composite 28-32

Name:	**University of Notre Dame**
Location:	**Notre Dame, Indiana**
Website:	**www.nd.edu**
US News & World 2012:	**19**
QS Ranking 2012:	**235**
THE Ranking 2011-12:	**89**
Admission Profile:	Need-aware
Cost of attendance:	$56,800 (2013-2014)
Tuition element of cost:	$43,000
Admission rate:	24%
Admission deadline:	December 31
	November 1 for merit scholarship
Scholarship deadline:	November 1
Common App®:	Yes
Advanced credit:	Higher IB

International student financial support:

Financial aid opportunities for first-year international students are limited. Based upon a review of academic qualifications, financial need, and availability of student aid resources, an applicant may be considered for financial assistance, including a self-help component of a student loan and student employment along with University scholarship assistance. The Certification of Finances and the International Student Financial Aid Application will be reviewed along with the student's application for admission.

Financial Documentation required

Notre Dame International Student Certification of Finances and International Student Financial Aid Application submitted as part of application for admission. Bank confirmation required that funds exist for all four years.

The Hesburgh-Yusko Scholars Program

The Hesburgh-Yusko Scholarship Program is a comprehensive, merit-based scholarship program that seeks to attract, encourage, and equip extraordinary students who will have a transformational effect on the Notre Dame community, the Catholic Church, and the world. Scholars participate in four fully funded Summer Enrichment experiences, beginning the summer prior to their first year. These summer experiences offer Hesburgh-Yusko Scholars unparalleled opportunities to develop and explore passions outside of the classroom. They will travel the world, discover new interests, identify true passions, refine lifelong pursuits, and lay the groundwork for future careers. Award: $25,000 annually for up to four years, plus funded summer enrichment programmes. Number of awards: 25.

Freshman Profile Class of 2015

(Mid-50% average) 1370–1500 on the SAT   32–34 on the ACT

Name:	University of Pennsylvania
Location:	Philadelphia, Pennsylvania
Website:	www.upenn.edu
US News & World 2012:	5 (tied)
QS Ranking 2012:	12
THE Ranking 2011-12:	16
Admission Profile:	Need-aware
Cost of attendance:	$59,600 (2012-2013)
Tuition element of cost:	$43,738
Admission rate:	12%
Admission deadline:	January 1
Scholarship deadline:	n/a
Common App®:	Yes
Advanced credit:	Higher IB
	A and AS Level

International student financial support:
The University of Pennsylvania has limited need-based financial aid available for students who are not U.S. citizens or bona fide permanent residents of North America. The offer of admission for non-citizens is directly linked to the ability to meet expenses. In recent years, UPenn has offered an average of 45 aid awards to admitted international freshmen. Like other Ivy League schools, Penn does not award scholarships based on academic or athletic merit.

Financial Documentation required
All international applicants must submit the International Student Certification of Finances form with application for admission. Those applying for need-based support should also submit the Online CSS Profile or the International Student Financial Aid Application.

Freshman Profile Class of 2015
SAT: Critical Reading 670-750
SAT: Math 690-780
SAT: Writing 680-780
ACT Composite 31-34

Name:	**University of Pittsburgh**
Location:	**Pittsburgh, Pennsylvania**
Website:	**www.pitt.edu**
US News & World 2012:	**58 (tied)**
QS Ranking 2012:	**98**
THE Ranking 2011-12:	**59**
Admission Profile:	No need-based aid, n/a
Cost of attendance:	$45,325 (2012-2013)
Tuition element of cost:	$29,498
Admission rate:	56%
Admission deadline:	April 1
Scholarship deadline:	n/a
Common App®:	No
Advanced credit:	Higher IB

International student financial support:
University of Pittsburgh does not provide need-based or merit-based financial aid to international students.

Financial Documentation required
All international applicants must submit acceptable documentation of financial support for the program after admission.

Freshman Profile Class of 2015
Middle 50% Admitted SAT Range Math: 610-720
Middle 50% Admitted Critical Reading: 590-700
Middle 50% Admitted Writing: 590-690
ACT Composite Range 26-31

Name:	University of Rochester
Location:	Rochester, New York
Website:	www.rochester.edu
US News & World 2012:	35
QS Ranking 2012:	135
THE Ranking 2011-12:	81
Admission Profile:	No need-based aid, n/a
Cost of attendance:	$61,365 (2012-2013)
Tuition element of cost:	$42,270
Admission rate:	37%
Admission deadline:	January 1
	December 1 recommended for international applicants
Scholarship deadline:	same as admission
Common App®:	Yes
Advanced credit:	Higher IB

International student financial support:
University of Rochester does not provide need-based financial aid to international students. To be eligible for admission students must demonstrate the ability to cover the estimated cost of at least one year of attendance at the time of application. All admitted undergraduate applicants, regardless of citizenship, are considered for merit scholarships.

Financial Documentation required
International Financial Support Form and supporting documents submitted as part of application for admission.

Merit Scholarships
All admitted undergraduate applicants are considered for merit scholarships. Scholarships are awarded to students who demonstrate outstanding academic achievement and potential, regardless of financial circumstances. Scholarships are awarded during the admission process and renewed annually if satisfactory academic performance is maintained. Each student is eligible to receive only one scholarship. Scholarships are awarded based on a variety of factors such as the rigor of the secondary school curriculum, academic achievement, excellent SAT scores, activity in a variety of extracurricular pursuits and a demonstrated understanding of the University of Rochester. Awards: from $5,000 to $15,000.

Renaissance and Global Scholarship
Renaissance and Global Scholars are an exceptional group of more than 80 students who come to Rochester from across the United States and all around the world. Not only are they academic all-stars, but they also have unique backgrounds that add to

the diversity of the student body and extraordinary life experiences that enhance the classes in which they are enrolled. Award: full tuition

International Baccalaureate Scholarship

Winners have excelled in one of the most rigorous college preparatory programmes available. This award is an acknowledgment of their hard work and determination. Award: starting at $7,000.

Mock Trial and Model United Nations Scholarships

Winners of Mock Trial and Model United Nations (MUN) Scholarships are academically excellent students who have a history of participation and leadership in these worldwide debate programmes. This is a reward for a student's hard work in high school and an investment in their continued success on campus. Award: starting from $10,000.

Freshman Profile Class of 2015

Middle 50% range for Enrolled Students

SAT Critical Reading 600-700

SAT Math 650-740

SAT Writing 610-700

ACT Composite 28-32

Name:	University of San Diego
Location:	San Diego, California
Website:	www.sandiego.edu
US News & World 2012:	97 (tied)
QS Ranking 2012:	not listed
THE Ranking 2011-12:	33
Admission Profile:	No need-based aid, n/a
Cost of attendance:	$57,163 (2012-2013)
Tuition element of cost:	$39,970
Admission rate:	48%
Admission deadline:	January 15
Scholarship deadline:	January 15
Common App®:	Yes
Advanced credit:	Higher and Subsidiary IB

International student financial support:
USD does not provide need-based financial aid to international students. International applicants are automatically considered by the Office of Admissions for merit scholarships. Students who do not receive a scholarship when admitted to USD cannot obtain one at a later stage. SAT/ACT not required for international applicants unless they want to be considered for merit scholarships.

Financial Documentation required
USD's Certificate of Finances and supporting documents submitted after admission.

Merit Scholarships
Awards are made based on superior academic achievement and test scores. The awards are renewable for eight semesters (10 semesters for engineers) provided the student satisfies the academic requirements. There is no separate application process. Awards: $5,000 to $20,000 per year. The number of awards varies, but scholarships are usually offered to top 35% of freshman applicant pool.

Freshman Profile Class of 2015
25th percentile 75th percentile
SAT Critical Reading 560 650   SAT Math 570 670
SAT Writing 570 660   ACT Composite 26 30
ACT English 25 31   ACT Math 25 30

Name:	University of Southern California
Location:	Los Angeles, California
Website:	www.usc.edu
US News & World 2012:	23 (tied)
QS Ranking 2012:	134
THE Ranking 2011-12:	55
Admission Profile:	No need-based aid, n/a
Cost of attendance:	$58,026 (2011-2012)
Tuition element of cost:	$44,468
Admission rate:	18%
Admission deadline:	January 10
	December 1 for scholarship consideration
Scholarship deadline:	December 1
Common App®:	Yes
Advanced credit:	Higher IB and A-levels

International student financial support:
USC does not provide need-based financial aid to international students. The financial support document, stating your ability to pay for the first academic year of tuition and expenses, must be verified by a bank and dated within the last year. Applicants who are relying on support from their home government or other official agency must send USC a similarly appropriate financial support document from their sponsor. It is crucial for applicants to submit their financial support documents with their applications if they wish to receive notification of admission in a timely manner. International students are eligible for merit-based scholarships.

Financial Documentation required
Financial Statement of Personal or Family Support submitted with application for admission. USC offers merit scholarships to international students. Candidates are selected by USC faculty and staff from an extremely competitive pool of international students. Students will have pursued the most demanding curriculum and achieved at the highest level. Average SAT and ACT scores are in the top 1–2 percent of all students. In addition to academic criteria, candidates' talent, involvement and leadership are considered.

Mork Family Scholarship
An interview is required for finalist candidates.
Award: full tuition approx. $45,000, plus a $5000 stipend

Trustee Scholarship
An interview is required for finalist candidates. Award: full tuition, approx. $45,000
Number of awards is approx. 100.

Presidential Scholarship

An interview is required for finalist candidates. Award: Half tuition, approx. $21,000. Number of awards: 200.

International Freshman Academic Scholarship

Competitive candidates will be at the top of the USC applicant pool with respect to SAT scores, will typically be in the top 10 percent of their high school classes, and will have extensive experience of living and studying outside the United States. To be considered students should submit a completed 2012 Common Application and USC Supplement by December 1. No additional application is required. Award equals half tuition, approx. $24,000. The number of awards varies.

International Freshman Deans Scholarship

Competitive candidates will be at the top of USC's applicant pool with respect to SAT scores, typically be in the top 10 percent of their high school class, and will have extensive experience of living and studying outside the United States. To be considered students should submit a completed 2012 Common Application and USC Supplement by December 1. All supporting documents, including proof of financial support, should be submitted by early January. No additional application is required. Award: One quarter tuition (approx. $10,000). The number of awards varies.

Freshman Profile Class of 2015

Middle 50%

SAT-Critical Reading 640-740

SAT-Math 680-770

SAT-Writing 670-760

ACT Composite 30-34

Name:	The University of Texas at Austin
Location:	Austin, Texas
Website:	www.utexas.edu
US News & World 2012:	45 (tied)
QS Ranking 2012:	68
THE Ranking 2011-12:	29
Admission Profile:	No need-based aid, n/a
Cost of attendance:	$50,990 (2012-2013)
Tuition element of cost:	$34,490
Admission rate:	47%
Admission deadline:	December 1
Scholarship deadline:	n/a
Common App®:	No
Advanced credit:	Higher IB

International student financial support:
UT Austin does not provide need-based or merit-based financial aid to international students. Proof of can be submitted once a student has been admitted. Once an international student is attending The University of Texas at Austin and has established an outstanding academic record, it may be possible to apply for scholarships through individual academic departments. Awards are based on academic achievement, but the availability of these funds is very limited.

Financial Documentation required
Online Certification of Financial Responsibility form and supporting documents submitted after admission.

Freshman Profile Class of 2015
Mid 50% SAT range: 1680 – 2020   SAT Average: 1844
Average SAT: Critical Reading: 602, Maths: 638   Writing: 604
Mid-50% ACT range: 25 – 31   ACT Average: 28
International Students: SAT: 1814   ACT Composite: 26

Name:	The University of Tulsa
Location:	Tulsa, Oklahoma
Website:	www.utulsa.edu
US News & World 2012:	75 (tied)
QS Ranking 2012:	601+
THE Ranking 2011-12:	not listed
Admission Profile:	No need-based aid, n/a
Cost of attendance:	$46,859 (2012-2013)
Tuition element of cost:	$32,410
Admission rate:	39%
Admission deadline:	Rolling applications but priority deadline February 1
Scholarship deadline:	February 1
Common App®:	Yes
Advanced credit:	IB and A Level
	IB Diploma students with a total score of 28 points or more will be awarded at least 30 hours of university credit (sophomore standing).

International student financial support:
The University of Tulsa does not provide need-based financial aid to international students. The University offers very limited merit scholarship assistance to international freshmen. All qualified applicants are automatically considered for merit scholarships as long as they complete their application for admission by February 1. Early application is recommended for the best chances of a scholarship.

Financial Documentation required
Tulsa's confirmation of resources form submitted with application for admission.

International Baccalaureate Scholarship
All entering freshmen who have fully participated in the IB Diploma are eligible. Award: $3,000 per year. The number of awards varies.

Richard C. Hojel Scholarship
This scholarship is available to Mexican students enrolling in the Petroleum Engineering programme at University of Tulsa. All qualifying applicants will be considered. No additional application is required. Award: full tuition, which is renewable. The number of awards varies.

Freshman Profile Class of 2015
ACT average: 28; ACT mid 50%: 24-31
SAT average: 1270; SAT mid 50%: 1140-1380

Name:	University of Vermont
Location:	Burlington, Vermont
Website:	www.uvm.edu
US News & World 2012:	82 (tied)
QS Ranking 2012:	451-500
THE Ranking 2011-12:	not listed
Admission Profile:	No need-based aid, n/a
Cost of attendance:	$49,524 (2011-2012)
Tuition element of cost:	$32,528
Admission rate:	71%
Admission deadline:	January 15
Scholarship deadline:	January 15
Common App®:	Yes
Advanced credit:	Higher IB and A Level

International student financial support:
UVM does not provide need-based financial aid to international students. International undergraduate applicants are automatically considered for several merit scholarships. Awards are made based upon all materials and information supplied with the application for admission to UVM.

Financial Documentation required
I-20 Request Form which includes sponsor declaration, and supporting documents submitted after admission.

Merit Scholarships for International Undergraduates
There is no separate application process and all international undergraduate applicants are considered. Scholarships are awarded based on their academic achievements supplied during the application process. These awards are very competitive and are renewable for four years. A cumulative 2.5 G.P.A. and full-time status is required to remain eligible for these scholarships.

International Distinction Scholarship
Award: $10,000 per year, renewable.

International Excellence Scholarship
Award: $8,000 per year, renewable.

International Recognition Scholarship
Award: $2,000 per year, renewable. The number of awards varies.

Freshman Profile Class of 2016
Middle 50% of Admitted Students

SAT Critical Reading: 560-670	SAT Math: 570-670
SAT Writing: 560-670	ACT composite: 26-30

Name:	University of Virginia
Location:	Charlottesville, Virginia
Website:	www.virginia.edu
US News & World 2012:	25 (tied)
QS Ranking 2012:	123
THE Ranking 2011-12:	135
Admission Profile:	No need-based aid, n/a
Cost of attendance:	$51,098 (2011-2012)
Tuition element of cost:	$36,788
Admission rate:	33%
Admission deadline:	January 1
	December 1 for Arts supplement
Scholarship deadline:	varies
Common App®:	Yes
Advanced credit:	Higher IB
	A and AS Level

International student financial support:

University of Virginia does not provide need-based financial aid to international students. Unless an international applicant is offered a merit scholarship, he or she must satisfy the requirements of the Financial Guarantee Form to demonstrate that the cost of attending can be met.

Financial Documentation required

Financial Guarantee Form must be submitted by January 1. This form includes Sponsors Affidavit of Support. Supporting documents must include verification of sponsor's earnings, bank statement or letter showing total funds available. UVA states that international students must provide documentation to prove financial capability to meet all anticipated expenses for all years of study.

The Jefferson Scholarship

See chapter five

The School of Engineering and Applied Science Awards

The School of Engineering and Applied Science considers all foreign nationals who apply to the School of Engineering for these scholarships. Recipients typically present above-average verbal SAT I scores and excellent SAT I math scores as well as excellent SAT II scores in math and one or more sciences. They are students at the top of their classes who have also demonstrated a depth of interest in engineering (through coursework, research, or science and math-related activities) and also show evidence of leadership or school citizenship. Scholarships are awarded primarily on the basis of academic merit, though financial need is sometimes used as a tie-breaker. These scholarships are renewable for four years provided the student remains in an engineering major and maintains at least a 3.0 grade-point average. Award: half the value of in-state tuition. Number of awards: four.

Freshman Profile Class of 2015

25th / 75th Percentile

SAT Critical Reading 610 720   SAT Math 630 740

SAT Writing 620 720   SAT Essay 8 10

ACT Composite 28 32   ACT Math 27 33

ACT English 28 34   ACT Writing 26 31

Name:	University of Wisconsin-Madison
Location:	Madison, Wisconsin
Website:	www.wisc.edu
US News & World 2012:	42 (tied)
QS Ranking 2012:	38
THE Ranking 2011-12:	27
Admission Profile:	No need-based aid, n/a
Cost of attendance:	$41,050 (2012-2013)
Tuition element of cost:	$26,630
Admission rate:	50%
Admission deadline:	November 1 first notification
	February 1 second notification
Scholarship deadline:	February 1
Common App®:	No
Advanced credit:	Higher IB

International student financial support:
UW-Madison does not provide need-based financial aid to international students. International applicants do not need to submit financial documents at the time of application. Once admitted students will need to complete and submit UW-Madison's Financial Verification Form.
International students can apply online for merit scholarships once they have received an application confirmation from UW-Madison.

Financial Documentation required
UW-Madison's Financial Verification Form submitted when admitted.

Merit Scholarships
Merit based aid is available but funds are limited and competition is strong. Once students have received an application confirmation they can complete the online scholarship application process. The scholarship application contains four sections: a demographic section, a recommendation section, an activities and accomplishments section, and an essay questions section.
Awards: $500 to $7,000 annually. Approximately 45 awards per year to freshmen students.

Freshman Profile Class of 2015
ACT Score: 27-31
SAT Score: 1860-2080

Name:	**University of Washington**
Location:	**Seattle, Washington**
Website:	**www.washington.edu**
US News & World 2012:	**42 (tied)**
QS Ranking 2012:	**59**
THE Ranking 2011-12:	**25**
Admission Profile:	No need-based aid, n/a
Cost of attendance:	$43,049 (2011-2012)
Tuition element of cost:	$27,830
Admission rate:	56%
Admission deadline:	December 1
Scholarship deadline:	n/a
Common App®:	No
Advanced credit:	Higher IB

International student financial support:

The UW does not provide need-based financial aid to international students. A Statement of Financial Responsibility is included in UW's online application and requires international students to show proof of finances for one full academic year at the time of applicaton. Once admitted, a bank confirmation of funding is required. International students and their families or sponsors must assume all responsiblity for student expenses. In recent years, UW has been able to offer admission to only half of the international students who have applied for admission. International applicants are not required to submit SAT or ACT exam scores, but are encouraged to do so.

Financial Documentation required

Statement of Financial Responsibility included in UW online application.

Freshman Profile Class of 2015

Middle 50%
SAT Critical Reading 510-650
SAT Math 570-700
SAT Writing 520-640
ACT Composite 24-30
ACT English 24-30
ACT Math 25-31

Name:	Vanderbilt University
Location:	Nashville, Tennessee
Website:	www.vanderbilt.edu
US News & World 2012:	17 (tied)
QS Ranking 2012:	167
THE Ranking 2011-12:	70
Admission Profile:	Need-aware
Cost of attendance:	$60,596 (2012-2013)
Tuition element of cost:	$41,088
Admission rate:	16%
Admission deadline:	January 3
Scholarship deadline:	Merit scholarships have earlier deadlines
Common App®:	Yes
Advanced credit:	Higher IB and A Level

International student financial support:

Vanderbilt University offers need-based financial aid to a limited number of international undergraduate applicants. Those international students who demonstrate they can afford the cost of attending Vanderbilt will be given preferential treatment in the admission process. By requesting consideration for need-based aid, admission to Vanderbilt is then "need-aware." International citizens who request need-based aid will be reviewed as a separate group and admission is more competitive. International freshmen applicants are eligible to apply for all Vanderbilt merit-based scholarships. Students must complete the appropriate application forms be either downloading the Vanderbilt Application Packet for merit-based Scholarships or completing the appropriate forms online.

Financial Documentation required

CSS Profile submitted with admission application if applying for need-based financial support.

Signature Scholarships

Vanderbilt has three Signature Scholarships. Approximately 250 recipients each year are guaranteed full-tuition awards plus summer stipends for study abroad, research or service projects.

Ingram Scholars

Ingram Scholars are awarded to students who plan to combine a professional or business career with an exceptional commitment to community service. The programme supports students who are committed to developing their personal roles in the solution to societal problems and who have the maturity and initiative to lead positive social change. Scholars are selected on the basis of commitment to community engagement, strength of personal character, and leadership potential. The selection committee reviews academic records, scholarship application essays,

187

service records, and two letters of recommendation. Ingram Scholar Finalists are also required to interview on campus with the selection committee. www.vanderbilt.edu/ingram.

Cornelius Vanderbilt Scholars

Cornelius Vanderbilt Scholars awarded to students who combine outstanding academic achievement with strong leadership and contributions outside the classroom. Scholars are selected on the basis of academic achievement, intellectual promise, and leadership and contribution outside the classroom. The selection committees review the entire application for freshman admission along with the Cornelius Vanderbilt Scholarship application.

Chancellor's Scholars

Chancellor's Scholars awarded to students with outstanding high school records who have worked to build strong high school communities by bridging gaps among economically, socially, and racially diverse groups and who have demonstrated significant interest in issues of diversity education, tolerance, and social justice. Scholars are selected on the basis of commitment to diversity, leadership, strength of character, and academic achievement. Strong candidates are intellectually curious and able to articulate their ideas clearly.

Additional Merit Scholarships

Vanderbilt offers a limited number of merit-based scholarships in amounts varying from $8,000 per year up to full-tuition. Candidates for these scholarships will be identified on the basis of academic achievement and fulfilment of any specific scholarships qualifications. Students wishing to ensure their consideration encouraged to submit the Cornelius Vanderbilt Scholarship application.

The Early-White International Scholarship

The Early-White International Scholarship provides assistance to undergraduate international students from the United Kingdom or European Union member countries enrolled in the College of Arts and Science based.

The Irene and Thomas Harrington International Scholarship

This scholarship provides financial assistance to international students enrolled full time in any of Vanderbilt's four undergraduate schools. Preference is given to students from France and then to students from the European Union.

The Hilppa A.K. Roby Scholarship

The Hilppa A.K. Roby Scholarship provides full-tuition support to undergraduate students from Finland.

Freshman Profile Class of 2016

SAT (CR + M) Middle 50% 1380 – 1550

SAT Critical Reading Middle 50% 680 – 770

SAT Math Middle 50% 700 – 780   SAT Writing Middle 50% 670 - 760

ACT Middle 50% 31 - 34

Name:	Virginia Polytechnic Institute and State University
Location:	Blacksburg, Virginia
Website:	www.vt.edu
US News & World 2012:	71 (tied)
QS Ranking 2012:	337
THE Ranking 2011-12:	251-275
Admission Profile:	No need-based aid, n/a
Cost of attendance:	$39,936 (2011-2012)
Tuition element of cost:	$24,480
Admission rate:	67%
Admission deadline:	February 15
	January 31 for engineering scholarship
Scholarship deadline:	January 31 for engineering scholarship
Common App®:	No
Advanced credit:	Higher IB and A Level

International student financial support:
Virginia Tech does not provide need-based financial aid to international students. There are very limited merit scholarships available to international students.

Financial Documentation required
Virginia Tech's Financial certification form for undergraduate international students and supporting documents submitted as part of application. Sponsor's letter and bank statements also required.

The Dean's Scholar & Davenport Scholarships
The Dean's Scholar and Davenport Leadership programmes are for incoming freshmen sponsored by the College of Engineering. International students are eligible to apply. Successful applicants will have strong academic credentials, outstanding community service and demonstrated leadership potential. SAT average 1500 (for math and critical reading sections only). There is one online application for both scholarships. Award: Dean's Scholars $5,000 annually; Davenport Scholars receive an amount equal to in-state tuition; both renewable for up to four years if 3.5 GPA maintained. Number of awards: 15 to 25 Dean's Scholars; 4 to 8 Davenport Scholars

Freshman Profile Class of 2015
SAT Scores
25th Percentile Math 570 Critical Reading 540
75th Percentile Math 670 Critical Reading 640

Name:	Wake Forest University
Location:	Winston-Salem, North Carolina
Website:	www.wfu.edu
US News & World 2012:	25 (tied)
QS Ranking 2012:	317
THE Ranking 2011-12:	162
Admission Profile:	No need-based aid, n/a
Cost of attendance:	$58,260 (2012-2013)
Tuition element of cost:	$43,200
Admission rate:	40%
Admission deadline:	January 1
	December 1 for merit-based scholarship consideration
Scholarship deadline:	December 1
Common App®:	Yes
Advanced credit:	Higher IB

International student financial support:
Wake Forest University does not provide need-based financial aid to international students. Unless a foreign national applicant is offered a merit , he or she must show sufficient financial support before the University will consider an applicant for admission. International students are eligible for WFU's four major merit-based scholarships. These are available to the entire applicant pool and are therefore highly selective. The regular application serves as the scholarship application.
SAT/ACT Optional
If you feel that your SAT or ACT with writing scores are a good indicator of your abilities, you may submit them and they will be considered in your admissions decision. If, however, you do not feel that your scores accurately represent your academic abilities, you do not need to submit them until after you have been accepted and choose to enroll. If you choose to submit your scores, score reports must be sent directly from the testing centers.
Financial Documentation required
WFU's Confidential Financial Information for International Applicants Form and supporting documents submitted as part of application for admission.
Nancy Susan Reynolds Scholarships
Nancy Susan Reynolds Scholars must be not only excellent students and promising scholars, but also creative. Successful applicants have pursued the most challenging curriculum and achieved grade point averages and SAT scores that place them in the top few percentage points in comparison to their peers (often in the top 1 percent of their class, with SAT-1 scores above 1500). Reynolds Scholars have typically been leaders in a variety of extracurricular pursuits and won recognition for their

interests at the regional, state, or national level. Reynolds Scholars are encouraged to apply for up to $3,000 for a research, study or travel project during each of three summers between first and senior years. They also receive an additional $500 for expenses related to a one semester on a WFU overseas programme. Award: full tuition, room and board plus $1,500 for personal expenses. Number of awards: up to six.

Graylyn Scholarship

This scholarship recognizes leadership and academic excellence, with funding provided by and in recognition of the Graylyn International Conference Center of Wake Forest University. Successful applicants have pursued the most challenging curriculum available to them and have achieved grade point averages and SAT scores that place them in the top few percentage points in comparison to their peers (often in the top 1 percent of their class, with SAT-1 scores above 1500). Graylyn Scholars have typically been leaders in a variety of extracurricular pursuits and won recognition for their interests at the regional, state, or national level. Graylyn Scholars are encouraged to apply for up to $3,000 for a research, study or travel project during each of three summers between first and senior years. They also receive an additional $500 for expenses related to a one semester on a WFU overseas programme. Award: full tuition, room and board plus $1,500 for personal expenses. Number of awards: one.

Guy T. Carswell Scholarships

Scholarships are awarded to students with outstanding qualities of academic promise, leadership, and talent. Successful applicants have pursued the most challenging curriculum available to them and have achieved grade point averages and SAT scores that place them in the top few percentage points in comparison to their peers (often in the top 1 percent of their class, with SAT-1 scores above 1500). Carswell Scholars have typically been leaders in a variety of extracurricular pursuits and won recognition for their interests at the regional, state, or national level. Carswell Scholars are encouraged to apply for up to $3,000 for a research, study or travel project during each of three summers between first and senior years. They also receive an additional $500 for expenses related to a one semester on a WFU overseas programme. Award: full tuition, room and board plus $1,500 for personal expenses. Number of awards: up to six.

Joseph G. Gordon Scholarships

Wake Forest awards Joseph G. Gordon Scholarships to students who show exceptional promise and achievement and who are members of constituencies traditionally underrepresented at Wake Forest. Gordon Scholars are encouraged to apply for up to $3,000 for a research, study, or travel project during each of the three summers between the first and senior years. Gordon Scholars may also receive an extra $500 allowance for expenses related to one semester at a Wake

Forest overseas program. Award: tuition, room, and board, plus $1,500 for personal expenses.

Freshman Profile Class of 2015

25th /75th Percentile

SAT Critical Reading 610 700

SAT Math 620 700

ACT Composite 28 32

Name:	Washington University in St. Louis
Location:	St. Louis, Missouri
Website:	www.wustl.edu
US News & World 2012:	14
QS Ranking 2012:	84
THE Ranking 2011-12:	41
Admission Profile:	Need-aware
Cost of attendance:	$63,205 (2012-2013)
Tuition element of cost:	$42,500
Admission rate:	21%
Admission deadline:	January 15
Scholarship deadline:	January 15 for merit scholarships
Common App®:	Yes
Advanced credit:	Higher IB and A Level

International student financial support:
Washington University provides need-based financial assistance for freshman international students. Financial assistance for qualified students is considered on a case-by-case basis but funding is limited and it is not always possible to meet every recipient's requirements. Financial assistance is renewable for each year of undergraduate study, as long as the student is making normal progress toward the degree and maintaining a good academic record. International students are eligible to apply for merit-based scholarships. Finalists for most merit scholarships will be invited to visit Washington University for an interview and related activities. Washington University will pay for finalists' round-trip expenses once within the United States.

Financial Documentation required
CSS Profile or Washington University Family Financial Profile for International Applicants (International FPP) submitted for consideration for need-based financial support by February 1. Admitted students submit WU's Declaration and Certification of Finances.

College of Arts & Sciences: Honorary Scholars Program
The College of Arts & Sciences awards academic scholarships to incoming for each of the four years of study, as long as the Scholars are making satisfactory progress toward a Bachelor's degree. Honorary Scholars applicants may apply for one of four scholarships.

Arthur Holly Compton Fellowships in Physical Sciences and Mathematics Program
For students who plan to pursue undergraduate majors in earth and planetary sciences, environmental science, mathematics, or physics.

Award: Up to four full-tuition fellowships with a $1,000 stipend in physical sciences and mathematics annually. Number of awards: up to four.

George E. Mylonas Scholarships in Humanities Program

For students who plan to pursue undergraduate majors in Arabic; art history and archaeology; Chinese; classics/ancient studies; comparative arts; comparative literature; dance; drama; English; film and media studies; French; German; modern Hebrew; history; interdisciplinary project in the humanities; literature and history; Italian; Japanese; Jewish, Islamic, and Near Eastern studies; music; philosophy; religious studies; Russian studies; or Spanish. Award: full-tuition fellowships with a $1,000 stipend annually. Number of awards: up to four.

Florence Moog Fellowships in Biological Sciences and Chemistry Program

For students who plan to pursue undergraduate majors in biochemistry and molecular biology, biology, or chemistry. Award: full-tuition fellowships with a $1,000 stipend annually. Number of awards: up to four.

Arnold J. Lien Scholarships in Social and Behavioral Sciences Program

For students who plan to pursue undergraduate majors in African and African-American studies; American culture studies; anthropology; archaeology; economics; education; international and area studies; philosophy-neuroscience-psychology; political economy; political science; psychology; urban studies; or women, gender, and sexuality studies. Award: full-tuition fellowships with a $1,000 stipend annually Number of awards: up to four.

Liselotte Dieckmann Scholarship Program

Up to 16 Honorary Scholars Program scholarship applicants are named Liselotte Dieckmann Scholars. No additional application required.
Award: half-tuition scholarships in the College of Arts & Sciences.
Number of awards: up to 16.

Howard Nemerov Writing Scholars Program

The Howard Nemerov Writing Scholarships are designed for students with a true dedication to writing and exceptional writing talent. Scholars participate in a series of educational experiences designed to meet the needs and interests of writers, including enrollment in the Howard Nemerov Writing Seminar, submission of their work to campus publications, attendance at and participation in writing-intensive group activities, and the earning of a minor in English writing. Award: $3,000 annually. Number of awards: up to 10 each year.

J. Stephen Fossett Pathfinder Fellowship

Applicants for the Compton or Moog Fellowships may be considered for the Fossett Pathfinder Fellowship if they are interested in environmental studies.
Award: full-tuition fellowship with research stipend. Number of awards: one.

College of Architecture - James W. Fitzgibbon Scholarship in Architecture

Awarded to a freshman who plans to pursue a Bachelor of Science in Architecture degree or a Bachelor of Arts degree with a major in architecture.
Award: full-tuition fellowship with a $1,000 stipend annually
Number of awards: one plus up to five $6,000 awards to remaining finalists.

College of Art - The Fred Conway Scholarship and the Esther & Arthur Proetz Scholarship

Awarded in alternating years. All freshman applicants to the College of Art are eligible for these scholarships. No separate scholarship application is required; each College of Art applicant who submits a slide or digital portfolio will be considered for that year's scholarship. Award: full-tuition. Number of awards: one plus up to five $6,000 awards to remaining finalists.

Olin Business School - The Dean's Scholarship in Business

Incoming first-year undergraduate students seeking a Bachelor of Science in Business Administration degree may apply for the Dean's Scholarship. The scholarship is awarded for four years of study as long as the student is making satisfactory progress toward the degree. The scholarship recognizes first-year applicants to the Olin Business School who demonstrate outstanding character, academic achievement, and promise for a career in business. Award: full-tuition Number of awards: one plus several partial-tuition scholarships.

School of Engineering & Applied Science: Engineering Scholarship Programs

The Engineering Academic Fellowships recognize first-year applicants to the School of Engineering who demonstrate outstanding academic achievement, particularly in science and mathematics. Finalists will be selected based on academic achievement, leadership ability, research or other creative experience, contributions to school and community, written and spoken communications, recommendations, and potential for professional achievement.

Alexander S. Langsdorf Fellowships

Awarded to entering freshmen who demonstrate outstanding academic achievement, particularly in science and mathematics.
Award: full-tuition. Number of awards: up to four.

Calvin M. Woodward Fellowships

Awarded to entering freshmen who demonstrate outstanding academic achievement, particularly in science and mathematics.
Award: half-tuition fellowships. Number of awards: up to eight.

James M. McKelvey Undergraduate Research Award

This award supports research expenses and salary for working with any faculty member in engineering, medicine, or science. McKelvey Research Scholars may take advantage of special programming and mentoring throughout their undergraduate

career in addition to participating in a research seminar during the spring semester of their freshman year. McKelvey Research Scholars are encouraged to spend at least one summer in St. Louis engaged in research.
Award: $5,000 Number of awards: up to eight.

Entrepreneurial Scholars Program
High school seniors are invited to apply if they possess creativity, energy, and an entrepreneurial spirit that strives to translate their visions into enterprises, both profit and nonprofit, to benefit the community. Applicants may pursue any undergraduate major. Each student who applies should include a résumé of activities demonstrating his or her creative spirit and vision, as well as a strong commitment to entrepreneurship. Award: $3,000 annually.
Number of awards: up to 8 each year.

Annika Rodriguez Scholars Program
The university is seeking students of exceptional merit who demonstrate academic and leadership achievements and who have engaged in or shown a commitment to community service. Applicants should demonstrate their commitment to, or a history of, bringing diverse groups together and celebrating the cultures of diverse people. Awards: Multiple partial-tuition scholarships and multiple full-tuition scholarships with $2,500 stipends.

Freshman Profile Class of 2016
SAT Math 710-790 range of middle 50%
SAT Critical Reading 680-750 range of middle 50%
SAT Writing Not reported
ACT Composite 32-34 range of middle 50%

Name:	Worcester Polytechnic Institute
Location:	Worcester, Massachusetts
Website:	www.wpi.edu
US News & World 2012:	62 (tied)
QS Ranking 2012:	601+
THE Ranking 2011-12:	not listed
Admission Profile:	Need-aware
Cost of attendance:	$56,522 (2012-2013)
Tuition element of cost:	$41,230
Admission rate:	59%
Admission deadline:	February 1
Scholarship deadline:	March 1
Common App®:	Yes
Advanced credit:	Higher IB and A Level

International student financial support:
WPI offers limited need-based financial assistance to international students. WPI does not guarantee to meet applicants' full financial need. Financial assistance is only offered to international students who enter as freshman in the fall semester. Financial assistance should be considered secondary to family, government, and other sponsor support for the student's studies. Students must demonstrate a minimum family contribution of $15,000 to cover all living expenses, as well as funds for travel expenses, to be considered for financial assistance. International students are eligible for academic merit scholarships. It is possible to receive both Merit and International Scholarships but there are very few combined awards available.

Financial Documentation required
Students not applying for need-based financial support submit the WPI Certification of Finances Document and supporting sponsor documents at time of application for admission.
Students applying for need-based financial support should submit the International Student Financial Aid Application with their application for admission. They can choose to submit the WPI Certification of Finances Document with their application for admission or to submit the form along with their enrolment form at a later date.

Academic Merit Scholarships
Academic merit scholarships are offered to freshman applicants based on academic performance in high school, standardized test scores, leadership, extracurricular involvement and community service. All applicants for admission are automatically considered for merit scholarships. No additional applications are required but students wishing to strengthen their candidacy for the WPI specialty merit scholarships should submit the optional WPI Merit Scholarship Supplement Form.

Award: between $12,500 and $25,000 annually. The number of awards varies.

IB Diploma Scholarship

IB diploma graduates with a diploma score of 40 of greater admitted to WPI are guaranteed an academic merit scholarship. Award: at least $20,000, renewable. The number of awards varies.

International Scholarships

Need-based scholarships are offered to a limited number of international students. In order to apply for an International Scholarship, students must complete the International Student Financial Aid Application. The scholarships are based upon financial need, the student's academic profile, and any special talents or experiences that the student will bring to WPI. Awards: range between $5,000 to $25,000 annually. Number of awards: varies

Freshman Profile Class of 2015

25th Percentile 75th Percentile

SAT Critical Reading 560 670

SAT Math 640 730

SAT Writing 560 660

ACT Composite 27 31

Name:	Yale University
Location:	New Haven, Connecticut
Website:	www.yale.edu
US News & World 2012:	3
QS Ranking 2012:	7
THE Ranking 2011-12:	11
Admission Profile:	Need-blind
Cost of attendance:	$59,580 (2012-2013)
Tuition element of cost:	$42,300
Admission rate:	7%
Admission deadline:	December 31
Scholarship deadline:	n/a
Common App®:	Yes
Advanced credit:	Higher IB and A Level

International student financial support:
Yale's financial aid policies for foreign citizens are exactly the same as those for U.S. citizens: need-blind admissions and need-based aid. "Need-blind" means that Yale College admits students without regard to their ability to pay. "Need-based" means that financial aid packages are based on individual needs assessments, not based on merit awards. International students are evaluated using a needs analysis that takes into account the relative differences between the US economy and the economy of students' home countries. Yale will meet 100 percent of the demonstrated financial need with a combination of tuition grants and term-time employment. All financial aid is awarded on the basis of demonstrated financial need, there are no academic, athletic, or merit-based awards.

Financial Documentation required
Students applying for need-based financial support should submit the online CSS Profile, parents tax returns for previous year and Yale's International Non-Custodial Parent Statement.

Freshman Profile Class of 2015
Scores for tests are represented as low score | average score | high score
SAT I Verbal: 700 | 750 | 800
SAT I Math: 700 | 740 | 780
SAT Combined: 2,090 | 2,225 | 2,360
ACT Composite: 30 | 32 | 34

Name:	Yeshiva University
Location:	New York, New York
Website:	www.yu.edu
US News & World 2012:	45 (tied)
QS Ranking 2012:	241
THE Ranking 2011-12:	154
Admission Profile:	Need-aware
Cost of attendance:	$45,000 (2012-2013)
Tuition element of cost:	$35,500
Admission rate:	62%
Admission deadline:	February 1
Scholarship deadline:	February 1
Common App®:	No
Advanced credit:	Higher IB and A Level

International student financial support:
International students are eligible for financial assistance from Yeshiva University which may include a grant, a student loan or both. International students may be awarded a Yeshiva loan of up to $8,000 for the year in addition to any grants that they will be receiving. All international applicants are interviewed by a YU Admissions officer.

Freshman Profile Class of 2014
SAT 25/75 percentile
SAT 1100-1300

9. More scholarships for international students

The scholarships listed below are offered by various organisations to undergraduate students applying to US institutions. Students from all over the world are invited to apply. They are listed in alphabetical order. Please note that details may change and each applicant should check the corresponding website for deadlines and the most up-to-date information.

Alexander Graham Bell Association for the Deaf and Hard of Hearing

http://nc.agbell.org/NetCommunity/Page.aspx?pid=493

Students who were diagnosed with hearing loss before the age of seven are eligible for a merit-based scholarship ranging from $1,000-$10,000.

Armenian Students Association of Americas, Inc.

http://www.asainc.org/index.php

Full-time students of Armenian ancestry are eligible to apply for scholarships of $500 to $1,500 per year.

BMI Student Awards

http://bmi.com/foundation/

A series of scholarships for various music and art related fellowships and awards. Some geographical restrictions may apply. Deadlines vary.

Davis-Putter Scholarships

http://www.davisputter.org/

Need-based grants to undergraduate students actively working for peace and justice on campus or in their community.

Eurasian Undergraduate Exchange Program (UGRAD)

http://www.irex.org/programs/ugrad/index.asp

Fellowships to first, second, and third-year undergraduate students from Armenia, Azerbaijan, Belarus, Georgia, Kazakhstan, Kyrgyzstan, Moldova, Russian Federation, Tajikistan, Turkmenistan, Ukraine, and Uzbekistan. The programme supports one year of undergraduate study in the United States in a subject area similar to the subject students are studying in their home country.

Finlandia Foundation National Trust Scholarship

http://www.finlandiafoundation.org/Scholarships

Scholarships are available for full-time undergraduate and graduate students of all academic disciplines enrolled in accredited schools in the United States and Finland. Candidates must have achieved sophomore or higher status prior to receiving the award and must have maintained a 3.0 GPA.

The Fulbright Program

http://foreign.fulbrightonline.org/

Educational exchanges that strengthen understanding and communication between the United States and students from 140 countries. Students interested in applying for the Fulbright Student Program must apply through the Fulbright Program Office in their home country.

Hellenic Times Scholarship Fund

http://www.htsfund.org/guidelines.html

For enrolled undergraduate and graduate students of Greek descent, between the ages of 17 and 25. Scholarships will be awarded on the basis of necessity and merit.

Humane Studies Fellowships
http://www.theihs.org/humane-studies-fellowships
Humane Studies Fellowships are awarded to graduate students and outstanding undergraduates embarking on liberty-advancing careers. The fellowships support study in a variety of fields, including economics, philosophy, law, political science, history, and sociology. Fellowship awards range between $2,000 and $15,000.

John Bayliss Radio Scholarship
http://www.beaweb.org/bayliss/radio.html
The Bayliss Foundation has been distributing scholarships to outstanding broadcast students for over 23 years. Each award is for $5,000. The number of scholarships awarded each year depends on the size of the endowment.

King Faisal Foundation Scholarship
http://www.advance-africa.com/King-Faisal-Foundation-Scholarships.html
Funding opportunity for up to three years for Muslim students in medicine, engineering, and the sciences (physics, chemistry, and geology), for study at an accredited North American or European university.

The Margaret McNamara Memorial Fund (MMMF)
http://www.mmmf-grants.org/grants-us.html
For students from developing countries who are currently studying in the United States or Canada, the MMMF awards grants of approximately $12,000 each. Grants are not renewable.

Mayo Summer Undergraduate Research Fellowship (SURF) Program
http://www.mayo.edu/mgs/surf.html
$5000 research fellowships for undergraduate students dedicated to scientific research alongside professional biomedical scientists.

Microsoft Scholarships
http://www.microsoft.com/college/scholarships

Various scholarships for undergraduate students interested in computer science and related technical disciplines. Microsoft offers four different types of technical scholarships to current undergraduate students: General Scholarships, Women's Scholarships, Minority Scholarships and Scholarships for Students with Disabilities.

Open Society Institute (OSI) Individual Fellowships and Scholarships
http://www.soros.org/grants

Provides support for fellowships, scholarships and related activities that empower individuals throughout the world to improve the social, political, and intellectual environments of their home communities.

Society of Women Engineers
http://www.societyofwomenengineers.org/scholarships/brochure.aspx
Various awards for women pursuing Bachelor's or Master's degrees in engineering or computer science with preference given to those students in ABET-accredited engineering programmes.

Statens Lanekasse for Utdanning
http://www.lanekassen.no/Toppmeny/Languages/
Provides educational grants and loans for Norwegian students abroad. Applicants must be in at least their sophomore year of undergraduate study.

Student Academy Awards
http://www.oscars.org/saa/
Awards and cash grants offered for students making films which are judged in four categories: animation, documentary, narrative and alternative. An outstanding student filmmaker from outside the US is honoured each year.

Swiss Benevolent Society of New York Scholarships

http://www.sbsny.org/sbs_scholarships.html

Merit based awards for study at the undergraduate, graduate and professional levels both in the US and abroad. The applicant or one of his or her parents must be a Swiss national.

Swiss Friends of the USA

http://www.sfusa.ch/

The Society of Swiss Friends in the USA scholarship award of CHF 25,000 is awarded to 6 to 8 applicants who have a connection to Switzerland and wish to progress with their education in the US.

United States-South Pacific Scholarship Program (USSP)

http://www.eastwestcenter.org/education/student-programs/opportunities-study/us-south-pacific-scholarship

Students from South Pacific island nations (Cook Islands, Fiji, Kiribati, Nauru, Niue, Papua New Guinea, Samoa, Solomon Islands, Tonga, Tuvalu, and Vanuatu) who, are not US dual citizens or permanent residents, and have completed high school can apply for this competitive merit based scholarship for undergraduate study in the US. Priority is given to students wishing to pursue Associate's or Bachelor's degrees in agriculture, business, computer science, education, environmental studies, journalism, political science and public administration. The scholarship includes a summer internship in Washington D.C. as well as a community service project in the recipient's home country. It is expected that four scholarships will be awarded to commence studies for the 2013 academic year.

United States - Timor-Leste Scholarship Program

http://www.eastwestcenter.org/education/student-programs/opportunities-study/us-timor-leste-scholarship

East Timorese students who have completed high school can apply for this competitive merit based scholarship for undergraduate study in the US. Priority is given to students wishing to pursue Associate's or Bachelor's degrees in fields that are relevant to the development needs of the country, including agriculture, business, communication, computer science, economics, education, environmental sciences, international relations, political science, psychology and urban planning. The scholarship includes one year of intensive English language training, a summer internship in Washington D.C. as well as a community service project in Timor-Leste. It is expected that four scholarships will be awarded to commence studies for the 2013 academic year.

Glossary

Articulation agreements - Agreements between two schools or institutions that contractually allow the transfer of credit from one institution to the other. These agreements are often between a community college and a nearby university.

Associates degree - a degree awarded by junior or community colleges after completion of a two-year programme.

Class - A meeting of a group of students for instruction, or a specific year of university, typically the graduation year i.e. Andrew is a member of the class of 2015.

College - A school within a university (Spanish is taught in the College of Arts & Sciences) or a stand-alone, academic institution (The College of William & Mary).

College Board - A for-profit organisation that manages various tools used by US universities for the purpose of admission. Specifically for undergraduates, tools include the SAT exam and the College Scholarship Service (CSS) Profile.

Common Application - Web-based admissions application system allowing students to apply online to over 400 US institutions. www.commonapp.org.

Cost of Attendance (COA) - The overall cost to attend an institution. For financial aid purposes, the COA is used to determine need in the equation, COA-EFC = need. The COA is made up of many elements including tuition, accommodations, food, books, personal expenses and insurance.

College Scholarship Service (CSS) Profile - A financial profile used by universities to determine both the estimated family contribution (EFC) and overall ability of the student to meet their university financial obligations. Institutions will collect financial information on the family income, assets, tax returns, past tuition payments and number of other children, usually through CollegeBoard.org©. Some institutions will offer their own family financial profile for international applicants as an alternative to the CSS Profile.

Credit – Earned for the successful completion of academic courses. While credits will vary between institutions typically 1 credit hour is the equivalent of approximately 15 'contact' hours, or classroom time, of course instruction. Therefore a 3 credit course is typically equivalent to approximately 45 hours spent in the classroom during the semester. Each institution will determine the total number of credits needed to graduate.

Degree - A title conferred on students by a college, university or professional school on completion of a program of study.

Dorms – Shortened from dormitories, or halls of residence, typically on campus.

Early action – an admissions process that requires students to submit an admission application before the standard deadline. Students are then notified earlier of the institution's admission decision. Restrictive early action is a binding agreement that restricts the student to applying to one institution and accepting admission if offered a place. Non-restrictive early action generally has no restrictions.

Electives – Classes that a student can choose independent of any general education requirements or major. Students can generally enrol in any class in any subject, providing the prerequisites for the class are met.

Endowment - The total value of an institution's investments. An institution's endowment is typically used for student scholarships, capital investments and other major projects, in accordance with the mission of the university.

Estimated Family Contribution (EFC) –the amount of money the family will put towards the cost of attendance for a university student. This amount is calculated differently at each institution. Institutions use formulas and financial details (often from the CSS Profile) to determine a family's ability to meet the university financial obligations of their student. The EFC and student contribution are used to determine need-based aid.

Faculty - The group of professionals who teach and conduct research on a US campus.

F-1 Visa - The US visa granted to most international undergraduate students attending a US university. Students must prove financial ability to support themselves in order to qualify for this visa. Funding from the university in the form of scholarships or aid typically does count towards the required ability to pay required by the US government.

Finals - End of term exams.

Financial aid - A broad term to describe funding received by students to assist in meeting their university financial obligations. Financial aid comes in many forms.

Fraternity/Sorority - A national male/female student club or society associated together in an environment of companionship and brotherhood/sisterhood. On US university campuses fraternities and sororities typically have a fraternity or sorority house or place of residence and names are designated by Greek letters, hence they are sometimes referred to as the Greek system.

Freshman - First year students.

Full-ride award - A merit-based scholarship that covers all of the costs of attending he institution, including tuition, room& board, books, university fees and insurance.

Full-time - A classification of a student attempting a specific amount of credits. Typically full-time students must take a minimum of three or four three credit classes earning at least 9 credits in a quarter system or 12 credits in a semester system.

General education requirements - a collection of classes required by an institution for graduation and serve as the basis for a Liberal Arts education. Classes in English, social sciences, history and foreign languages are often part of this requirement. Each institution will require its own set of required classes. Also known as GenEd's, core requirements or foundation classes.

GPA - Grade point average- GPA is calculated by taking the number of grade points a student earned in a given period of time divided by the total number of credits taken.

Grants - Grants are typically dispersed to students by governments to aid in the research or study of a specific discipline or research area. For example, the Fulbright Awards are grants to students studying and performing research around the world.

International English Language Testing System (IELTS) - One of the English language exams necessary for entrance into a US university for all international students where English is not the accepted native language of one's home country.

International Student Identity Card (ISIC) - A free card issued to international students for discounts on various goods and services. www.isic.org.

Ivy League - Eight of the oldest and most prestigious universities in America. Located in the Northeast part of America, these institutions are private and highly competitive. Brown University, Columbia University, Cornell University, Dartmouth College, Harvard University, University of Pennsylvania, Princeton University and Yale University make up the Ivy League.

Junior - A third year student.

Major – An area of study or discipline on which a student concentrates their studies. Students at US institutions usually declare a major in their second year of studies. (i.e. Sheila majored in Engineering at Iowa State University).

Merit-based aid - Financial assistance awarded to a successful applicant based on a particular skill, talent or achievement. Athletics, intelligence or musicianship are all reasons merit-aid may be awarded. Merit-based aid is also often called scholarships. These do not need to be repaid.

Need-aware - Institutions and universities who assess an admission application aware of an applicant's/families' resources to meet their university financial obligations. For example, Tufts University is a need-aware institution.

Need-based aid - Monies awarded to a student unable to meet their university financial obligations (i.e. the applicant shows need). Awarded by need-aware and need-blind institutions. Repayment requirements vary. An example of need-based aid is funding from Harvard University awarded to a new student.

Need-blind - Institutions and universities who assess an application for admission unaware of an applicant's/families' resources to meet their university financial obligations. For example, Amherst College is a need-blind institution.

Personal statement - A unique writing sample submitted to a university answering a particular question(s) or explaining the unique qualities possessed by an applicant. These statements are often required by universities.

President - Vice-Chancellor or head of the university.

Professor - Lecturer, generally holding a PhD.

Provost - Pro-Vice-Chancellor or Director of a college

Quarter – A ten-week academic term when classes and exams take place. Universities on the quarter system have three quarters during an academic year which full-time students attend: Fall, Winter and Spring.

Scholarships - A general term used to identify monetary awards offered by organisations and institutions to students dedicated to earning a higher degree or qualification. They can be full or partial and typically do not need to be repaid. There are many kinds of scholarships.

Semester –A 16-week academic term when classes and exams take place. Universities on the semester calendar have two semesters during an academic year which full-time students attend: Fall and Spring.

Senior - A fourth/final year student.

Sophomore - A second year student.

Specialty scholarships - These scholarships originate from various interest groups, ethnic societies and companies. The BMI Award, The Ayn Rand Essay contest and the Armenian Student Association are good examples of this category.

Student Visa - See F1 visa.

TOEFL- Test of English as a Foreign Language. English language exams necessary for entrance into a US university for all international students where English is not the native language of a student's home country.

Tuition - Fees charged by institutions for academic instruction.

Valedictorian - Student in the class with the highest GPA or grades.

Varsity - The term used to signify the best sports team on campus. Varsity level teams represent the university in conference play in a variety of sports.

Notes

Chapter 1 Introduction

U.S. Department of Education, 2011. *National Center for Education Statistics.* Available at: http://nces.ed.gov/fastfacts/ display.asp?id=76. [September 2012].

Chapter 2 What does a US university offer?

Gillespie, J. 2002. *Longitudinal Alumni Survey, IES Abroad Chicago IL.* Available from: https://www.iesabroad.org/IES/About_IES/IES_News/Articles/ newsArticle0033.html [April 2012].

TSL Education Ltd. 2012. *THE World University rankings 2011-2012.* Available from: http://www.timeshighereducation.co.uk/world-university-rankings/ [August 2012].

Institute of International Education. (2011). *Top 25 Places of Origin of International Students, 2009/10-2010/11.* Open Doors Report on International Educational Exchange. Available from http://www.iie.org/opendoors. [March 2012].

Harvard University. (2009). *The Task Force on General Education.* Available from: www.admissions.college.harvard.edu/about/learning/liberal_art s.html [January 2012].

University of California, Berkeley. (2012). *"Why study the Liberal Arts".* Available from: ls.berkeley.edu/about-college/liberal-arts-education. [January 2012].

University of North Carolina at Chapel Hill. (2012). *The 2012-2013 Undergraduate Bulletin*. Available from: http://www.unc.edu/depts/econ/undergraduate/majoring.htm. [December 2011].

Beloit College. (2012) *Clubs and Greeks*. Available at: http://www.beloit.edu/studentlife/clubsandgreeks/ [February 2012].

Georgia Institute of Technology (2012). *About Us*. Available at: http://www.crc.gatech.edu/plugins/content/index.php?id=111 [March 2012].

Chapter 3 What type of institution is best for you?

National Center for Education Statistics (2011). *Number of educational institutions, by level and control of institution: Selected years, 1980-81 through 2008-09, Table 5*. Available at: http://nces.ed.gov/programs/digest/. [October 2011].

The Regents of the University of Michigan. (2012). *General University Timeline*. Available at: http://bentley.umich.edu/exhibits/umtimeline/general.php [December 2012].

Carey, Kevin (2009) Built to Teach. *What your alma mater could learn from Cascadia Community College*. Washington Monthly, June 2007 Available at: http://www.washington monthly.com/features/2007/0709.careycascadia.html. [October 2011].

Miami-Dade College (2012) *Funeral Services Education*. Available at: http://www.mdc.edu/north/funeralsciences/ default.asp. [December 2011].

American Association for Community Colleges. (2012) *About AACC*. Available at: http://international.aacc.nche.edu /about/Pages/default.aspx [September 2012].

U.S. Department of Education (2012). *Accreditation in the U.S.* Available at: www2.ed.gov/admins/finaid/accred/accreditation pg2.html#U.S. [November 2011].

National Junior College Athletic Association. (2012). Available at: http://www.njcaa.org/marketing.cfm. [November 2011].

National Collegiate Athletic Association. (2012). Available at: www.ncaa.org/wps/wcm/connect/public/ncaa/eligibility/index.h tml. [November 2011].

Memphis Journal. (2012). Available at: http://www.bizjournals.com/memphis/news/2012/08/29/combi ned-revenue-of-15-richest-college.html. [September 2012].

The New York Times Company. (2012). Available at: http://collegefootball.about.com/od/stadiums/a/stadiumsrank.h tm [August 2012].

Chapter 4 Admissions and financial aid overview

Duke University (2009). Available from: http://admissions.duke.edu/application/aid#foreign-nationals. [November 2012].

University of Pennsylvania. (2009). Available from: http://www.sfs.upenn.edu/paying/paying-grants-scholarships.html. [November 2012].

Chapter 5 Full-merit based scholarships

Angier B. Duke Memorial Scholarship Program. (2012). Available at: http://abduke.duke.edu/about/. [October 2012].

American University. (2012). *The AU Emerging Global Leader Scholarship for International Students.* (2012). Available at:http://www.american.edu/admissions/international/egls.cfm [July 2011].

Grinnell College. (2012). *International Student Financial Aid.* Available at: http://www.grinnell.edu/admission/apply international/finaid/. [September 2012].

The Jefferson Scholars Foundation. (2012). *The Jefferson Scholarship.* Available at: www.jeffersonscholars.org. [1994-2011].

Davidson College. 2012. *John Montgomery Belk Scholarship.* Available at: www3.davidson.edu/cms/x27480.xml. [March 2012].

The Morehead-Cain. (2003-2011). *About.* Available at: http://moreheadcain.org/about. [March 2012].

The Trustees of Boston College. (2012). *Presidential Scholars Program.* Available at: http://www.bc.edu/centers/psp/. [March 2012].

Villanova University. (1993-2012). *Presidential Scholarships.* Available at: http://www1.villanova.edu/villanova/ admission/presidentialscholarships.html. [March 2012].

The Robertson Scholars Program. (2005). *The Program.*
Available at: www.robertsonscholars.org. [March 2012].

Boston University Admissions. (2012). *Trustee Scholarship.*
Available at: www.bu.edu/admissions/apply/costs-aid-
scholarships/scholarships/trustee. [March 2012].

Chapter 6 Other notable aid opportunities or programmes

Colby College. (2012). *The Oak Institute for International
Human Rights.* Available at: http://web.colby.edu/oak/oak-
scholarships/ [March 2012].

The Cooper Union for the Advancement of Science and Art.
(2012). *Mission and Vision.* Available at:
http://cooper.edu/about/mission-vision. [August 2012].

Davis United World College Scholars. (2012). *Global
Engagement on US campuses.* Available at:
www.davisuwcscholars.org. [March 2012].

Emory University. (2012) *Emory Scholars Program.* Available
at: http://college.emory.edu/home/academic/scholar.
[March 2012].

Franklin & Marshall College. (2012). *International Student
Admission.* Available at:
http://www.fandm.edu/apply/international-student.
[August 2012].

Jack Kent Cooke Foundation. (2008). *Undergraduate Transfer
Scholarship.* Available at: http://www.jkcf.org/scholarships/
Undergraduate-transfer-scholarships/ [June 2012].

Lynn University. (2012). *Lynn 3.0*. Available at:
www.lynn.edu/academics/other-academic-
programs/accelerated-degree-programs/lynn-3.0. [March 2012].

Marquette University. (2012) *International Undergraduate
Scholarships*. Available at:
http://www.marquette.edu/oie/intl_scholarships.shtml. [March
2012].

Oberlin College. (2012). *Finances for International Students*.
Available at: http://new.oberlin.edu/arts-and-
sciences/admissions/finances/international-students.dot.
[August 2012].

Oregon State University. (2012). *Financial aid and Scholarships*.
Available at: http://oregonstate.edu/international
/atosu/scholarships. [May 2012].

Saint John's College. (2012). *International Admissions*. Available
at: http://www.stjohnscollege.edu/admissions/
international.shtml. [March 2012].

Smith College (2012). *Financial Aid*. Available at:
http://www.smith.edu/finaid/prospect/aid_merit.php
[August 2012].

Swarthmore College. (2012). *Financial Aid*. Available at:
http://www.swarthmore.edu/cc_financialaid.xml.
[August 2012].

Tulane University. (2012). *International Student Financial Aid*.
http://admission.tulane.edu/international/intlscholarships.php
[August 2012].

University of Portland. (2012). *International Student Services: Financial Resources.* Available at: http://www.up.edu/show image/show.aspx?file=4025. [December 2011].

Vassar College.(2012). *Financial Aid.* Available at: http://admissions.vassar.edu/finaid.html. [May 2012].

Wesleyan University. (2012*). Freeman Asian Scholar Program.* Available at:http://www.wesleyan.edu/admission/ international_students/freeman.html. [May 2012].

Chapter 7 Scenarios to reduce cost

Duke University. (2012) *Advance Placement.* Available at: http://admissions.duke.edu/application/instructions#credit-and-advanced-placement. [July 2012].

Stanford University. (2012). *Language Requirement.* Available at: https://www.stanford.edu/dept/lc/language/requirement/. [August 2011].

The College Board. (2008) *Annual Survey of Colleges.* Figures obtained by subtracting average published tuition and fees for public two-year schools ($2,402), from that of public four-year ($6,585) and private four-year ($25,143) schools. These relative annual savings amount to $4,183 between public two-year and public four-year schools, and $22,741 between public two-year and private four-year schools. Available at: http://professionals. collegeboard.com/higher-ed/recruitment/annual-survey [May 2011].

Northern Virginia Community College. (2012). Available at: http://www.nvcc.edu/about-nova/directories-offices/administrative-offices/academic/guaranteed-adm/index.html. [July 2012].

Northern Virginia Community College. (2012). *Tuition & Fees.* Available at: http://www.nvcc.edu/future-students/paying-for-college/tuition-fees/ [July 2012].

CUNY Borough of Manhattan Community College (2012) *Articulation Agreements.* Available at: http://www.bmcc.cuny.edu/news/news.jsp?id=5073 [September 2011].

Miami-Dade College (2012). *Articulation Institutions.* Available at: http://www.mdc.edu/asa/popups/institution_list2.asp [December 2011].

United States Digest of Educational Statistics, *The Condition of Education,* (Washington: NCES, 1992).

University of California. (2012). *UC Office of the President.* Available at: http://www.ucop.edu/news/factsheets/fall2010adm.html. [June 2012].

Truman State University. (2012). *About Truman.* Available at: http://about.truman.edu/facts2.asp [March 2012].

US Department of Labor. (2011*) Wage and Hour Division.* Available at: http://www.dol.gov/whd/minwage/america.htm [May 2011].

Chapter 8 Financial assistance available for international students from the top-ranked US universities

US News & World 2012 refers to the ranking service provided by The US News & World Report. Available here: http://colleges.usnews.rankingsandreviews.com/best-colleges/rankings/national-universities. [September 2012].

QS Ranking 2012 refers to the World University Rankings provided by QS Quacquarelli Symonds Limited 1994-2011. Available here: http://www.topuniversities.com/university-rankings/world-university-rankings/2012. [September 2012].

THE Ranking refers to the Times Higher Education World University Rankings service provided by Time Higher Education (published by TSL Education Ltd.). Available here: http://www.timeshighereducation.co.uk/world-university-rankings/. [September 2012].

CommonApp refers to the Common Application. A free online application supplied by The Common Application, Inc. Available here: https://www.commonapp.org/CommonApp/default.asp. [September 2012].

U.S. Department of Education (2012). Accreditation in the U.S. Available at: www2.ed.gov/admins/finaid/accred/accreditation_pg2.html#U.S. [November 2011].

Appendix 1
Web resources for scholarships

There are literally hundreds of sites that explain and list scholarships available to international students. Like many websites, some of them are legitimate and others are not. The list below is a good starting point for international students seeking financial assistance.

> If you come across a website that requests credit card information or payment upfront, leave the website immediately. No true academic scholarship will ask for a pre-payment or a credit card.

For another glossary of terms, go here:
http://www.edupass.org/english/glossary.phtml

www.internationalscholarships.com
A general but relatively easy scholarship website that does not require a lot of information. These pages of scholarships will need to be carefully vetted.

www.iie.org/en/program-finder
A reputable source for various scholarship programmes throughout the world. Designate as many criteria as necessary.

www.fundingusstudy.org
As above, another source from the Institute of International Education.

www.scholarshipexperts.com
Another search engine. It does ask for a little information but the website then delivers scholarships for which you can apply.

Appendix 2

Accreditation

"The United States has no federal Ministry of Education or other centralised authority exercising single national control over postsecondary educational institutions in the country. Each state assumes varying degrees of control over their education provision, but, in general, institutions of higher education are permitted to operate with considerable independence and autonomy. As a consequence, American educational institutions can vary widely in the character and quality of their programs". (US Department of Education 2012).

The six main accrediting commissions for post-secondary institutions are:

- Middle States Commission on Higher Education
- New England Association of Schools and Colleges
- North Central Association of Schools and Colleges
- Northwest Commission on Colleges and Universities
- Southern Association of Colleges and Schools
- Western Association of Schools and Colleges

All of the schools mentioned in this book are accredited. US accrediting agencies set goals for educational institutions and assess whether an institution has reached those goals. This accreditation process:

- Confirms to students that the education will be of a high quality and consistent with the standards set in other countries.

- Helps the US government identify institutions with respect to funding.

- Creates a consistent level of quality throughout the country and allows for credit transfer between institutions.

Appendix 3

General university costs

Listed below are some of the standard costs that are usually required by an international student at a US institution. For reference, the 2010-2011 academic year, the annual average tuition for a US public institution was $13,600 and $36,300 at a US private institution. (U.S. Department of Education, 2011).

Application costs

Submission of a US application	$50-$125 per application
SAT I exam	$50 each
SAT II subject exams	$50 each
ACT exam	$50 each
SAT / ACT Study guide	approx. $20 + shipping
CSS Profile	$25.00 for the first, $16 to each additional university

Attendance costs

Tuition	$0 to $45,000 per year
Housing	$2,350 to $13,590 per year
Food (depends on student)	$2,500 and $3,500 per year
Books	$400 to $2000 per year
Insurance (required)	$300 to $800, depending on coverage and university

Visa fees (required)	Visa processing fee - $140
	SEVIS F-1 fee - $200
	Issuance fee, $0 -$200

Other costs to consider include flights, currency exchange fees, clothes, a computer, postage, tickets for sporting events & concerts and other personal items.

Most US universities also offer payment plans for international students. Students can often spread their payments over a specific period of time as dictated by the university. Customer service is highly regarded in the States, so it is suitable to inquire about optional payment schedules or plans. A fee may be involved.

About the Author

Steve Fenoglio has more than 20 years of professional experience in international higher education. Steve's professional roles have included academic advising, international recruitment, admissions and programme development. He is now the Managing Director of Mayflower Education Consultants Ltd.

Originally from Chicago, Steve has a Master's degree in International Studies from DePaul University and Bachelor's degree from Miami University in Oxford, Ohio. He lives with his wife and cat in southeast England. His email is steve@mayflowereducation.co.uk